NIST Special Publication 800-79-1

NIST
National Institute of Standards and Technology
U.S. Department of Commerce

Guidelines for the Accreditation of Personal Identity Verification Card Issuers

Ramaswamy Chandramouli
Dennis Bailey
Nabil Ghadiali
Dennis Branstad

INFORMATION SECURITY

Computer Security Division
Information Technology Laboratory
National Institute of Standards and Technology
Gaithersburg, MD 20899-8930

June 2008

U.S. Department of Commerce
Carlos M. Gutierrez, Secretary

National Institute of Standards and Technology
James M. Turner, Acting Director & Deputy Director

Reports on Computer Systems Technology

The Information Technology Laboratory (ITL) at the National Institute of Standards and Technology (NIST) stimulates U.S. economic growth and industrial competitiveness through technical leadership and collaborative research in critical infrastructure technology, including tests, test methods, reference data, and forward-looking standards, to advance the development and productive use of information technology. To overcome barriers to usability, scalability, interoperability, and security in information systems and networks, ITL programs focus on a broad range of networking, security, and advanced information technologies, as well as the mathematical, statistical, and computational sciences. The Special Publication 800-series reports on ITL's research, guidelines, and outreach efforts in information system security, and its collaborative activities with industry, government, and academic organizations.

Authority, Usage, and Revisions

This document has been developed by the National Institute of Standards and Technology (NIST) in furtherance of its statutory responsibilities under Homeland Security Presidential Directive 12, signed August 27, 2004.

NIST is responsible for developing standards and guidelines, including specifying minimum requirements, for providing adequate information security for all organizational operations and assets, but such standards and guidelines shall not apply to national security systems. This guideline is consistent with the requirements of the Office of Management and Budget (OMB) Circular A-130, Section 8b(3), Securing Agency Information Systems, as analyzed in A-130, Appendix IV: Analysis of Key Sections. Supplemental information is provided A-130, Appendix III.

This document has been prepared for use by Federal agencies but it also may be used by non-governmental organizations on a voluntary basis. Nothing in this document should be taken to contradict standards and guidelines made mandatory and binding on Federal agencies by the Secretary of Commerce under statutory authority. This document should not be interpreted as altering or superseding the existing authorities of the Secretary of Commerce, Director of the Office of Management and Budget, or any other Federal official. This document is not subject to copyright but attribution for its adoption and use would be appreciated by NIST.

Comments may be submitted to the Computer Security Division,
Information Technology Laboratory, NIST
via electronic mail at PIVaccreditation@nist.gov
or via regular mail at

100 Bureau Drive
Mail Stop 8930
Gaithersburg, MD 20899-8930

Acknowledgments

The authors wish to thank their colleagues who contributed to this document's development and reviewed its many versions. We would especially like to thank Ron Martin from the Department of Health and Human Services; Kurt Kersch and Barry Colvin from the Department of Treasury, Internal Revenue Service; Miguel Calin from Mitre; Sarbari Gupta and Andrew Founds from Electrosoft Services; William MacGregor, Ketan Mehta, and Tanya Brewer from NIST, each for their technical inputs, Personal Identity Verification Card Issuer experience, SP 800-79-1 document preparation assistance, and editorial suggestions. The authors also gratefully acknowledge and appreciate the many comments and contributions made by government organizations, private organizations, and individuals in providing direction and assistance in the development of this document.

TABLE OF CONTENTS

EXECUTIVE SUMMARY 1

1. INTRODUCTION 3
   1.1 Applicability, Intended Audience, and Usage 5
   1.2 History of this Revision...5
   1.3 Timelines for using the revised Guidelines 6
   1.4 Key Related NIST Publications 6
   1.5 Organization of this Special Publication 7

2. THE FUNDAMENTALS 8
   2.1 PCI 8
   2.2 PCI Facilities 8
   2.3 Outsourcing of PCI Functions...9
   2.4 Assessment and Accreditation 10
   2.5 Accreditation Boundary for the PCI 11
   2.6 PCI Roles and Responsibilities 12
      2.6.1 Senior Authorizing Official 12
      2.6.2 Designated Accreditation Authority 12
      2.6.3 Organization Identity Management Official 12
      2.6.4 PCI Facility Manager 12
      2.6.5 Assessor 13
      2.6.6 PIV Card Applicant Representative 13
      2.6.6 Privacy Official 13
      2.6.7 Role Assignment Policies 13
      2.6.8 Accreditation-related PCI Roles 14
   2.7 The Relationship between SP 800-79-1 and SP 800-37 14
   2.8 Preparing for a PCI's Assessment 15
      2.8.1 PCI Duties.. 15
      2.8.2 Assessment Team Duties 16
   2.9 Accreditation Decisions..16
      2.9.1 Authorization to Operate 17
      2.9.2 Interim Authorization to Operate 18
      2.9.3 Denial of Authorization to Operate 18
   2.10 The Use of Risk in the Accreditation Decision 19
   2.11 Accreditation Submission Package and Supporting Documentation 19

3. PIV CARD ISSUER (PCI) COMPLIANCE 22
   3.1 Introducing PCI Controls 22
   3.2 Implementing PCI Controls 24
      3.2.1 PCI Controls implemented at the Organization or Facility Level 24

4. ASSESSMENTS 26
   4.1 Assessment Methods 27
   4.2 The Assessment Report 29

5.0 ACCREDITATION 32
   5.1 Initiation Phase 32

5.2 ASSESSMENT PHASE 35
5.3 ACCREDITATION PHASE 38
5.4 MONITORING PHASE 40

APPENDIX A: REFERENCES 43

APPENDIX B: GLOSSARY AND ACRONYMS 45

APPENDIX C: PCI READINESS REVIEW CHECKLIST 48

APPENDIX D: PCI OPERATIONS PLAN TEMPLATE 50

APPENDIX E: ASSESSMENT REPORT TEMPLATE 53

APPENDIX F: SAMPLE TRANSMITTAL AND DECISION LETTERS 55

APPENDIX G: PCI CONTROLS AND ASSESSMENT PROCEDURES 59

APPENDIX H: ASSESSMENT AND ACCREDITATION TASKS FOR PIV CARD ISSUERS (PCIs) 77

TABLES AND FIGURES

FIGURE 1 - OUTSOURCING OF PCI FUNCTIONS 9
FIGURE 2 - PCI ACCREDITATION ROLES 14
FIGURE 3 - ACCREDITATION SUBMISSION PACKAGE 21
TABLE 1 - PATS AND ASSOCIATED ACCREDITATION FOCUS AREAS 24
TABLE 2 - PAT, ACCREDITATION FOCUS AREA, AND PCI CONTROL RELATIONSHIPS 24
TABLE 3 - SAMPLE PCI CONTROLS WITH ASSESSMENT PROCEDURES 29
FIGURE 4 - SAMPLE ASSESSMENT REPORT 30
FIGURE 6 - ACCREDITATION PHASES 32

EXECUTIVE SUMMARY

Homeland Security Presidential Directive 12 (HSPD-12), dated August 27, 2004, established a policy for creation, issuance, and use of personal identification credentials in the Federal government. The Directive requires the development and use of a standard for a secure and reliable form of identification for Federal employees and contractors. The Personal Identity Verification (PIV) specifications of the resulting standard are to be used as a foundation for securely identifying every individual seeking access to valuable and sensitive Federal resources, including buildings, information systems, and computer networks. The implementation of PIV specifications will, in turn, involve operations such as the collection, access protection, and dissemination of large amounts of personal information, which itself requires privacy protection.

NIST developed and published the Federal Information Processing Standard (FIPS) 201-1, entitled *Personal Identity Verification of Federal Employees and Contractors,* as well as several NIST Special Publications (SPs) providing additional specifications and supporting information in response to HSPD-12. These documents provide the required foundation for standardizing the processes relating to adoption and use of government-wide personal identification credentials and the issuance of PIV smart cards as a means to verify the identity of the credential holders.

In light of the requirements for both improved security and protection of personal privacy, HSPD-12 established four control objectives, one of which includes the call for a form of identification that is "issued by providers whose reliability has been established by an official accreditation process." In response, Appendix B of FIPS 201-1 specified that NIST "…establish a government-wide program to accredit official issuers of PIV Cards…," which led to development of this NIST SP, entitled *Guidelines for the Accreditation of Personal Identity Verification Card Issuers.*

The purpose of this SP is to provide appropriate and useful guidelines for accrediting the reliability of issuers of Personal Identity Verification cards that are established to collect, store, and disseminate personal identity credentials and issue smart cards, based on the standards published in response to HSPD-12. These issuers, who are the target of assessment and accreditation, are called Personal Identity Verification Card Issuers or PCIs. The reliability of PCIs is of utmost importance when one organization (e.g., a Federal agency or Federal contractor) is required to trust the identity credentials and cards of individuals that were created and issued, respectively, by another organization. This trust will only exist if organizations relying on the credentials and cards issued by a given organization have the necessary level of assurance that the reliability of the issuing organization has been established through a formal accreditation process.

This SP provides an assessment and accreditation methodology for verifying that issuers of PIV credentials and cards are reliably adhering to standards and implementation directives developed under HSPD-12. The salient features of the methodology are:

(i) Controls derived from specific requirements in FIPS 201-1 and relevant documents for PCIs;

(ii) Procedures for assessing and monitoring adherence to the requirements through a determination of control implementation; and

(iii) Guidance for evaluating the result of an assessment in order to arrive at the accreditation decision.

Arriving at an accreditation decision that authorizes a PCI to operate establishes the reliability of that PCI.

Accreditation is one a basis for establishing trust of PCIs and requires that all assessment and accreditation processes be thorough and comprehensive. Careful planning, preparation, and commitment of time, energy, and resources are required. These guidelines are designed to assist agencies in creating the needed roles, assigning responsibilities, developing an acceptable operations plan, drawing a PCI's accreditation boundary, evaluating the findings of all reliability assessments, and making a proper decision for accrediting the PCI. Realizing that organizations may vary significantly in how they choose to structure their PCI operations, these guidelines have been developed to support organizational flexibility, and are designed to minimize the effort needed to assess, accredit, and monitor the continued reliability of a PCI.

In addition to flexibility and efficiency, the accreditation methodology defined in these guidelines generates assessment findings and resulting accreditation decisions that are consistent and repeatable. These characteristics provide assurance to an organization's management that when a PCI has been accredited based on these guidelines, the target of accreditation can be trusted as a provider of secure and reliable identification credentials as required by HSPD-12.

This document shall be used by both small and large organizations where processes performed by their PCIs relating to PIV Card issuance are:

- Centrally located;
- Geographically dispersed; or
- Outsourced in varying degrees to another organization(s) or service provider(s).

1. INTRODUCTION

In order to enhance security, increase Government efficiency, reduce identity fraud, and protect personal privacy, the President issued Homeland Security Presidential Directive 12 (HSPD-12), *Policy for a Common Identification Standard for Federal Employees and Contractors*, dated August 27, 2004. This Directive established a Federal policy to create and use a government-wide secure and reliable form of identification for Federal employees and contractors. It further defined *secure and reliable identification* as one that—

- Is issued based on sound criteria for verifying an individual's identity;
- Is strongly resistant to identity fraud, tampering, counterfeiting, and terrorist exploitation;
- Can be rapidly authenticated electronically; and
- Is issued only by providers whose reliability has been established by an official accreditation process.

NIST developed and published Federal Information Processing Standard (FIPS) 201-1, entitled *Personal Identity Verification (PIV) of Federal Employees and Contractors*, and several Special Publications providing additional specifications and supporting information in response to HSPD-12. These documents provide the foundation for Government personal identification, verification, and access control systems.

Appendix B.1 of FIPS 201-1 states the following:

"... [HSPD-12] requires that all cards be issued by providers whose reliability has been established by an official accreditation process. Funding permitting, NIST will establish detailed criteria that PIV Card Issuers must meet for accreditation. Additionally, NIST will (again, funding permitting) establish a government-wide program to accredit official issuers of PIV Cards against these accreditation criteria. Until such time as these are completed, agencies must self-certify their own issuers of PIV Cards..."

In order to satisfy HSPD-12 and FIPS 201-1, NIST undertook the development of the *Guidelines for the Certification and Accreditation of PIV Card Issuers* and published them as NIST Special Publication (SP) 800-79. This document is the first revision to the original. The revised SP 800-79-1 provides a more technically-based approach to assure that a PCI is fulfilling all the requirements of FIPS 201-1 and its supporting documents, and doing so reliably. In this revised document, a PCI is considered to be owned and managed by an *organization* which may be a Federal department, agency, state or local government, private entity, or other enterprise that desires to issue reliable PIV Cards. Ensuring the reliability of a PCI is of critical importance in light of the security and privacy implications of HSPD-12 and its far-reaching objective of issuing PIV Cards to millions of employees and contractors. HSPD-12 and its implementing standards and guidelines were developed to address a range of security concerns, including those posed by terrorists in a post-9/11 world. Providing a comprehensive set of standards for controlling access to the physical and logical resources through the use of a standard PIV Card assures that certain pre-defined levels of security can be achieved. However, it requires organizations to implement and use the standards in a consistent and reliable manner.

An organization must have confidence in the cards it issues to its own employees and contractors, but possibly more importantly, since HSPD-12 requires a common inter-operable standard, all organizations need to have confidence in the cards issued by other organizations. This confidence can come about only if the PCI functions in those other organizations are assessed and accredited. Thus, PCI accreditation forms an important task in meeting the end-goals of HSPD-12.

NIST has considerable experience in the development of accreditation methodology, most significantly with the widely accepted approach to accreditation in SP 800-37, *Guide for the Security Certification and Accreditation of Federal Information Systems,* and its family of related documents. While SP 800-37 is focused on the accreditation of the security of information systems, rather than the accreditation of the reliability of PCIs, it does offer a practical foundation for accreditation programs in general. This document utilizes various aspects of SP 800-37 and applies them to accrediting the reliability of PCIs. Accreditation of a PCI requires prior accreditation of the security of all information systems used by the PCI in accordance with SP 800-37.

One difference between the accreditation of the security of information systems and the accreditation of the reliability of a PCI is that an organization has considerable flexibility in how they prepare for a SP 800-37 accreditation (particularly in implementing security controls), but have little room for variation under SP 800-79-1. Much of the flexibility in SP 800-37 comes from the necessity of acceptable variations in security controls, since individual information systems within varied environments may have significantly different security requirements. Conversely, the desire for standardization that is implicit in HSPD-12 has led to the development of a stable set of requirements. There may be some flexibility in how a requirement is met, but a majority of requirements must be satisfied in a uniform manner in order to deem a PCI as reliable. Allowing too much latitude in how a requirement is met undermines this reliability.

Although organizations may feel constrained by the uniformity required by FIPS 201-1, standardization greatly contributes to achieving the objectives of HSPD-12 across PIV Card Issuer implementations. For all organizations to accept the PIV Cards of other organizations, one set of rules (i.e., FIPS 201-1) must be followed by all PIV system participants. This Special Publication provides a way of determining if the participants are following these rules. Accreditation efforts that are consistent, reliable, and repeatable provide a basis for determining the *reliability* and *capability* of providers who issue PIV Cards, which herein is defined as *consistent adherence to the PIV standards.* In particular, if PCIs meet the requirements of FIPS 201-1 and relevant documents as verified through applicable assessment procedures and maintain consistency of their operations with respect to meeting these criteria, they can be considered reliable as is required by HSPD-12.

The objectives of the guidelines in this document are to—

- Outline the requirements to be met by a PCI, the rationale for the requirements and the assessment procedures required to determine the satisfaction of those requirements by a PCI through a combination of policies, procedures, and operations.

- Describe an accreditation methodology that provides a framework for organizing the requirements and assessment procedures stated above and at the same time provides coverage for all the control objectives stated in HSPD-12.
- Demonstrate the fact that the application of the methodology will result in assessment outcomes that are consistent, reliable, and repeatable.
- Emphasize the role of risk in arriving at an accreditation decision, based on assessment outcomes that takes into account the organization's mission.

1.1 Applicability, Intended Audience, and Usage

This document is applicable to, and shall be used by, all Federal organizations for all their employees and contractors for authorizing their physical access to Federal facilities (e.g., buildings, leased offices) and logical access to Federal information systems. It may also be used by any other organization (e.g., state and local government, educational, non-profit) desiring compliance with FIPS 201-1.

All Federal organizations are required to adopt HSPD-12, implement FIPS 201-1, and use SP 800-79-1 to assess the adequacy of their implementations and accredit the reliability of the directly-controlled or sub-contracted services involved in creating and issuing PIV Cards. All non-Federal organizations (e.g., state governments) and private organizations specifying mandatory conformance with FIPS 201-1 in a procurement contract should use these guidelines to assess and accredit the services of their PIV Card Issuers.

SP 800-79-1 is consistent and compatible with HSPD-12, FIPS 201-1, and SP 800-37. SP 800-79-1 includes a number of roles, requirements, definitions, specifications, and procedures needed to adequately assess and accredit the reliability of a PIV Card Issuing organization (PCI). All PCIs should issue PIV Cards only after they have been authorized to operate based on this document. In situations where a PCI that has already started issuing cards fails a SP 800-79-1 accreditation, it must immediately halt operations. Similarly, if the PCI that has already started issuing cards obtains a SP 800-79-1 accreditation subject to some terms and conditions, those restrictions must be immediately enforced in its operations.

Once a PCI is accredited using the guidelines within this document, trust can be established in the PIV Cards it issues. However, organizations that accept PIV Cards issued by PCIs that are not accredited are doing so at their own risk, since no assurance has been obtained about the reliability of operations for those PCIs.

The keywords "MUST", "MUST NOT", "REQUIRED", "SHALL", "SHALL NOT", "SHOULD", "SHOULD NOT", "RECOMMENDED", "MAY", and "OPTIONAL" in this specification are to be interpreted as described in IETF RFC 2119.

1.2 History of this Revision

In order to satisfy HSPD-12, SP 800-79 was developed in July 2005, shortly after publication of FIPS 201, in order to provide organizations with an initial set of guidelines for accreditation of their PIV Card Issuers. While the original version had a clear idea of the functions needed for deployment of a PIV Card, it was impossible to foresee how the organization and management of these functions and the structuring of the PCI would evolve. The experience gained since then has provided the knowledge and perspective needed to develop a new accreditation methodology that is objective, efficient, and will result in consistent and repeatable accreditation decisions.

The major changes for this revision include:

- Removal of attributes as the basis of reliability assessment, and replacing them with PCI controls, traceable to specific requirements from FIPS 201-1 and related documents;
- Additional guidelines on how to determine the accreditation boundaries of a PCI;
- Discussion of the risk involved in authorizing the operation of a PCI;
- Removal of "Section 4.0 - PCI Functions and Operations" and "Section 5.0 - PIV Services and Operations," which were narrative discussions of FIPS 201-1 requirements;
- Clarification of the similarities and differences between the accreditation of computer systems for secure operation as specified in SP 800-37 and the accreditation of the reliability of an organization as specified in SP 800-79-1;
- Changing the term "certification" to "assessment"; and
- Use of "organization" instead of "department" or "agency."

1.3 Timelines for using the revised Guidelines

These revised guidelines for accrediting PCIs will take effect immediately following publication of SP 800-79-1. Hence, organizations shall use these revised guidelines for accrediting any new PCI, any PCI whose accreditation is currently in progress, or any PCI that previously has gone through accreditation (under SP 800-79) and failed (with or without being issued a Denial of Authorization to Operate (DATO) or Interim Authorization to Operate (IATO)). Any PCI that has already been accredited and currently holds the Authorization to Operate (ATO) under SP 800-79 must be re-accredited based on these revised guidelines no later than one year after the final publication date.

1.4 Key Related NIST Publications

The following NIST publications include a standard and supporting specifications and guidelines to organizations implementing HSPD-12, and were utilized as the basis for requirements listed in this document.

- FIPS 201-1, *Personal Identity Verification (PIV) of Federal Employees and Contractors*
- SP 800-37, *Guide for the Security Certification and Accreditation of Federal Information Systems*
- Draft SP 800-73-2, *Interfaces for Personal Identity Verification*
- SP 800-76-1, *Biometric Data Specification for Personal Identity Verification*
- SP 800-78-1, *Cryptographic Algorithms and Key Sizes for Personal Identity Verification*

- SP 800-85A, *PIV Card Application and Middleware Interface Test Guidelines (SP 800-73 Compliance)*
- SP 800-85B, *PIV Data Model Test Guidelines*
- SP 800-87, *Codes for Identification of Federal and Federally-Assisted Organizations*
- SP 800-104, *A Scheme for PIV Visual Card Topography*

1.5 Organization of this Special Publication

The remainder of this publication is organized as follows:

- **Chapter 2** provides background information needed to understand the PCI accreditation methodology, as well as the inputs and outputs involved in the assessment and accreditation processes. These include: (i) Definition of the target accreditation entities (PCI, PCI facilities, PCI boundaries); (ii) the relationship between accreditation under SP 800-37 and accreditation under SP 800-79-1; (iii) preparatory tasks of accreditation including assignment of roles and responsibilities; (iv) three alternative accreditation decisions; (v) acceptance of risk in the accreditation decision; and (vi) the contents of the accreditation package.

- **Chapter 3** describes the building blocks of the PCI accreditation methodology, including Accreditation Topics, Accreditation Focus Areas, and the control requirements within each area called PCI controls.

- **Chapter 4** provides a detailed description of the assessment methods for the PCI controls whose outcomes form the basis for the accreditation decision.

- **Chapter 5** describes the 4 phases of the accreditation methodology and the tasks involved in each phase.

- **Appendices** include— (i) references; (ii) glossary and acronyms; (iii) PCI readiness review checklist; (iv) PCI operations plan template; (v) assessment report template; (vi) sample accreditation transmittal and decision letters; (vii) PCI controls and assessment procedures; and (viii) summary of tasks and sub-tasks.

2. THE FUNDAMENTALS

This chapter presents the fundamentals of Personal Identity Verification (PIV) Card Issuer (PCI) accreditation including: (i) definitions of a PCI and a PCI Facility; (ii) outsourcing PCI services or functions; (iii) the differences between assessment and accreditation; (iv) accreditation boundaries of a PCI; (v) roles and responsibilities; (vi) the relationship between accreditation under Special Publication (SP) 800-37 and SP 800-79-1; (vii) preparing for the assessment; (viii) types of accreditation decisions; (ix) use of risk in the accreditation decision; and (x) the contents of the accreditation package.

2.1 PCI

At the highest level, a PCI includes all functions required to produce, issue, and maintain PIV Cards for an organization. A PCI is considered operational if all relevant roles and responsibilities have been defined and appointed; suitable policies and compliant procedures have been implemented for processes, including sponsorship, enrollment/identity proofing, adjudication, card production, card activation/issuance, and maintenance; and information system components that are utilized for performing the above-mentioned functions (processes) have been assessed and shown to meet all technical and operational requirements prescribed in FIPS 201-1 and related documents.

In order to comply with Homeland Security Presidential Directive 12 (HSPD-12), an organization must first establish a PCI that conforms to and satisfies the requirements of FIPS 201-1 and related documents. The PCI must then be accredited (i.e., using the guidelines specified in SP 800-79-1). An organization has certain flexibility in establishing a PCI. It may outsource some of the required processes within its PCI. Large organizations with widely varying missions for its operating units may even establish multiple PCIs. Regardless of how a PCI is structured, the organization (e.g., Federal agency, Federal contractor) is responsible for the management and oversight of the PCI and maintains full responsibility for the accreditation of the PCI as required in HSPD-12.

A PCI must be completely described in its PCI operations plan. This comprehensive document incorporates all the information about the PCI that is needed for any independent party to review it and assess the capability and reliability of the PCI's operations. A PCI operations plan includes a description of the structure of the PCI, its facilities, any external service providers, the roles and responsibilities within the PCI, policies and procedures which govern its operations, and a description of how requirements of FIPS 201-1 are being met. A template for a PCI operations plan is provided in Appendix D.

2.2 PCI Facilities

A PCI Facility (PCIF) is a physical site or location–including all equipment, staff, and documentation–that is responsible for carrying out one or more of the following PIV functions: (i) enrollment/identity proofing; (ii) card production; (iii) card activation/issuance; or (iv) maintenance. A PCIF operates under the auspices of a PCI, and implements the policies and executes procedures prescribed by the PCI for those functions sanctioned for the facility (e.g. an enrollment/identity proofing facility).

Based on certain characteristics (e.g. size, geographic locations, the organization(s) that it supports), a PCI may have its services and functions provided centrally or distributed across multiple locations. Independent of how or where a PCI implements these functions, at least one PCIF is required. For example, a geographically dispersed organization may decide to have enrollment/identity proofing and card activation/issuance functions performed in different facilities in different parts of the country so that applicants can minimize travel. In this example, the different PCIFs fall under the purview (policy, management) of a single PCI which encompasses all the functions necessary to issue PIV Cards. Within that PCI, the geographically dispersed PCIFs have specific responsibilities and are under the direct management control of the PCI.

2.3 Outsourcing of PCI Functions

An organization may out-source its PCI functions to one or more organizations. As the complexity and cost of new technology increase, the organization may decide that the most efficient and cost-effective solution for implementing HSPD-12 is to seek the services of an external service provider. An external service provider may be a Government agency, a private entity, or some other organization that offers services or functions necessary to issue PIV Cards.

Figure 1 provides an illustration of the functions that can be outsourced. Only the organization which "owns" (i.e., manages, controls, or privately owns) the PCI can decide which of its employees and contractors are required to apply for a PIV Card (Sponsorship – a responsible official of the organization providing the biographic and organizational affiliation of the PIV card applicant) and under what conditions the application will be approved (Adjudication – the kind of background information that will form the basis for authorization for PIV Card Issuance). Therefore, these two functions cannot be outsourced.

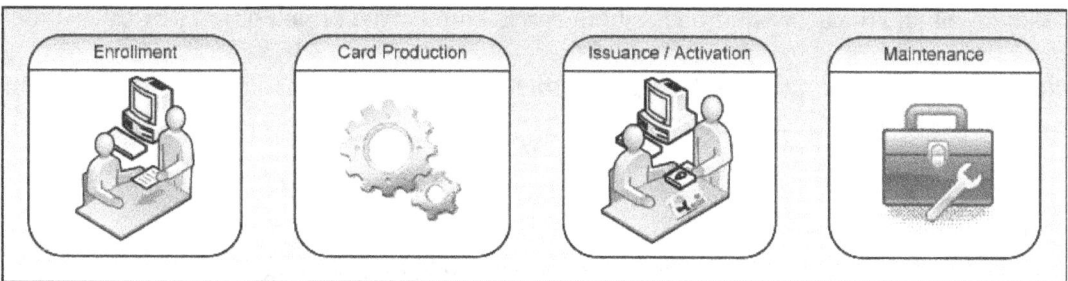

Figure 1 - Outsourcing of PCI Functions

A PCI which out-sources services to an external provider must make sure that all privacy-related requirements are satisfied. The PCI is responsible for ensuring that privacy requirements are being met both internally and by every external service provider.

If an organization's management is considering using the services of a PCI set up by another organization, the operations plan and associated documents, the accreditation decision and evidence of implementation of FIPS 201-1 requirements of that PCI (service provider PCI) must be reviewed. Similarly, if a PCI is using the services of an external service provider selectively for one or more of its PCI processes, the provider's capability to meet FIPS 201-1 requirements for those processes must be reviewed as well. In both cases, the information gathered as part of this review activity must be included as part of the PCI's assessment leading to accreditation. Outsourced functions must be assessed prior to accreditation of the PCI.

2.4 Assessment and Accreditation

HSPD-12 mandates that PIV Cards be "issued only by providers whose reliability has been established by an official accreditation process." This document contains guidelines for satisfying the requirements for an official accreditation and provides a methodology that any organization can utilize to formally accredit a PCI. This methodology consists of two major elements–assessment and accreditation. While assessment and accreditation are very closely related, they are two very distinct activities.

Assessment, which occurs before accreditation, is the process of gathering evidence regarding a PCI's satisfaction of the requirements of FIPS 201-1, both at the organization and facility level. Assessment activities include interviews with PCI and PCIF personnel, a review of documentation, observation of processes, and execution of tests to determine reliability of the PCI. The result of the assessment is a report that serves as the basis for an appropriate accreditation decision. The report is also the basis for developing corrective actions for removing or mitigating discovered deficiencies.

Distinct from assessment, accreditation is the decision to authorize the operation of a PCI once it has been established that the requirements of FIPS 201-1 have been met and the risks regarding security and privacy are acceptable. The individual making the accreditation decision must be knowledgeable of HSPD-12 and aware of the potential risks to the organization's operations, assets, and personnel (e.g., applicants, PCI Facility staff).

The assessment and the accreditation are both carried out by the organization that owns the PCI.

In order to make an informed, risk-based accreditation decision, the assessment process should seek to answer the following questions:

- Has the PCI implemented the requirements of FIPS 201-1 in the manner consistent with the standard?
- Do personnel understand the responsibilities of their roles and/or positions, and reliably perform all required activities as described in the PCI's documentation?
- Are services and functions throughout the PCI and its facilities (e.g., enrollment/identity proofing, card activation/issuance) carried out in a consistent, reliable, and repeatable manner?
- Have deficiencies identified during the assessment been documented, current and potential impact on security and privacy been highlighted, and the recommendations and timelines for correction or mediation been included in the assessment report?

2.5 Accreditation Boundary for the PCI

An organization preparing to accredit a PCI must first identify the appropriate accreditation boundary. The accreditation boundary defines the specific PCI operations that are to be the target of the assessment and accreditation. A PCI comprises the complete set of functions required for the issuance and maintenance of PIV Cards. In determining the accreditation boundary, the organization may consider if the functions are being performed identically in all PCI facilities, are using identical information technology components, and are under the same direct management control. For instance, an organization may have two sub-organizations, each of which has distinct processes and management structures. The organization may decide to establish two separate PCIs, each with its own accreditation boundary. In this example, two separate PCI assessments would be undertaken. Each assessment would result in an independent accreditation decision.

In drawing an accreditation boundary, an organization may want to include only a subset of PCI facilities. For example, if a PCI has several facilities, some of which are ready for operation and some that are still in the development stage, the organization may choose to define the accreditation boundary to include the PCI and only those facilities that are ready to be assessed. If the accreditation is successful, the PCI and a subset of its facilities will be authorized to operate and begin issuing cards. The remaining PCIFs can continue with implementation and be included in the accreditation boundary at a later date.

In the case of outsourcing PCI services that are not under direct management control of the organization nor physically located within its facilities, the organization must include the functions provided by external service providers within the accreditation boundary to make certain that they are included within the scope of accreditation. This assures that no matter how and where the functions are performed, the organization maintains complete accountability for the reliability of its PIV program.

Care should be used in defining the accreditation boundary for a PCI. A boundary that is unnecessarily expansive (i.e., including too many dissimilar processes and business functions or geographically dispersed facilities) makes the assessment and accreditation process extremely unwieldy and complex. On the other hand, a boundary that is unnecessarily limited increases the number of needed assessments and accreditations and thus drives up the total cost for an organization. Establishing a boundary for a PCI and its subsequent accreditation are organization-level activities that should include participation of all key personnel. An organization should strive to define the accreditation boundary for a PCI that strikes a balance between the costs and benefits of assessment and accreditation.

While the above considerations should be useful to an organization in determining the boundary for its PCI for purposes of accreditation, they should not limit the organization's flexibility in establishing a practical boundary that promotes an effective HSPD-12 compliant implementation. The scope of an accreditation is a PCI (whose boundaries are formed by included facilities) and not individual facilities (PCIFs).

2.6 PCI Roles and Responsibilities

FIPS 201-1 Appendix A provides examples of two models that satisfy the requisite PIV control objectives and meet the requirements for issuance of PIV Cards. An organization may select either of the two models, employ a hybrid, or utilize a completely new model. PIV Card issuance roles and their processes are to be selected based on the organization's structure, its mission, and operating environment. The organization must make sure that a separation of roles has been established and the processes are in compliance with FIPS 201-1.

Roles discussed in FIPS 201-1 pertain to PCI processes and functions, and are included by reference, but not defined in this document. This document identifies only roles and responsibilities of key personnel involved in the accreditation of a PCI[1]. Recognizing that organizations have widely varying missions and structures, there may be some differences in naming conventions for accreditation-related roles and in how the associated responsibilities are allocated among personnel (e.g. one individual may perform multiple roles).

2.6.1 Senior Authorizing Official

The Senior Authorizing Official (SAO) (see Figure 2) of an organization is responsible for all PCI operations. The SAO has budgetary control, provides oversight, develops policy, and has authority over all functions and services provided by the PCI.

2.6.2 Designated Accreditation Authority

The Designated Accreditation Authority (DAA) is an official of the organization with the authority to review all assessments of a PCI and its facilities, and to accredit the PCI as required by HSPD-12. Through accreditation, the DAA accepts responsibility for the operation of the PCI at an acceptable level of risk to the organization. The SAO can also fulfill the role of the DAA.

2.6.3 Organization Identity Management Official

The Organization Identity Management Official (OIMO) is responsible for implementing policies of the organization, assuring that all specified procedures of the PCI are being performed reliably, and providing guidance and assistance to the PCI Facilities. The OIMO implements and manages the PCI operations plan; ensures that all PCI roles are filled with capable, trustworthy, knowledgeable, and trained staff; makes certain that all PCI services, equipment, and processes meet FIPS 201-1 requirements; monitors and coordinates activities with PCI Facility Manager(s); and supports the accreditation process. The OIMO cannot fulfill the role of the DAA.

2.6.4 PCI Facility Manager

A PCI Facility (PCIF) Manager manages the day-to-day operations of a PCI facility. A PCIF Manager is responsible for implementing all operating procedures for those functions that have been designated for that facility. The PCIF Manager must ensure that all PIV processes adhere to the requirements of FIPS 201-1, and that all PIV services performed at the PCIF are carried out

---

[1] Organizations may define other significant roles (e.g., PIV System liaisons, operations managers) to support the PCI accreditation process.

in a consistent and reliable manner in accordance with the organization's policies and procedures and the OIMO's direction. In some cases (e.g. small organizations), the OIMO can fulfill the role of the PCIF Manager.

2.6.5 Assessor

The Assessor is responsible for performing a comprehensive and independent assessment of a PCI. The Assessor (usually supported by an assessment team) verifies that PIV processes in a PCI comply with control objectives of FIPS 201-1. The results of an assessment are presented to the OIMO who reviews the assessment findings and prepares recommended corrective actions to reduce or eliminate any discrepancies or shortcomings. The Assessor is also responsible for providing recommendations for reducing or eliminating deficiencies and security weaknesses, describing the potential impact of those deficiencies if not corrected. An Assessor cannot be assigned the DAA's role and vice versa.

To preserve the impartial and unbiased nature of the assessment, the Assessor must be independent of the office(s) and personnel directly responsible for the day-to-day operation of the PCI. The Assessor shall also be independent of those individuals responsible for correcting deficiencies and discrepancies identified during the assessment phase. The independence of the Assessor is an important factor in maintaining the credibility of the assessment results and ensuring that the DAA receives objective information in order to make an informed accreditation decision.

2.6.6 PIV Card Applicant Representative

The PIV Card Applicant Representative (CAR) is an optional role within the PCI and may be established and used at the discretion of the organization. The CAR represents the interests of current or prospective employees and contractors who are the applicants for PIV Cards. They are responsible for assisting an applicant who is denied a PIV Card because of missing or incorrect information, and for ensuring that all applicants obtain useful information and assistance when needed. This role may be assigned to someone in the organization's personnel or human resources department as part of their normal duties.

2.6.6 Privacy Official

The responsibilities of the Privacy Official (PO) are defined in FIPS 201-1. The person filling this role shall not assume any other operational role in the PCI. The PO issues policy guidelines with respect to collection and handling of personally identifiable information from applicants so as to ensure that the PCI is in compliance with all relevant directives of the privacy laws. The PO's role may be filled by an organization's existing official for privacy (e.g., a Chief Privacy Officer).

2.6.7 Role Assignment Policies

Although PCI roles are independent and should be filled by different people if feasible, there may be a need (e.g., because of availability or economy) to have one person fill more than one role. Except for the roles of Assessor and Privacy Official, one person may perform more than one role if needed. If an organization has multiple PCIs, one person may be assigned the same role in several or all of them. For instance, a SAO may be responsible for several PCIs within the organization. Similarly, within a single PCI, a PCIF Manager may be responsible for a number of PCI Facilities. Of the roles described, the SAO, DAA, OIMO, CAR, Assessor and PO must be employees of the organization that owns the PCI (e.g., Federal employees in the case of Federal agencies).

2.6.8 Accreditation-related PCI Roles

Figure 2 illustrates a possible role structure when a PCI has multiple PCIFs. The SAO has the primary authority and responsibility for the PCI. Reporting to the SAO are the OIMO and the DAA. A PCI Facility Manager is responsible for managing operations at each PCI facility and reports to the OIMO. The dotted lines leading to the PO and the Assessor indicate their independence from the day to day operations of the PCI.

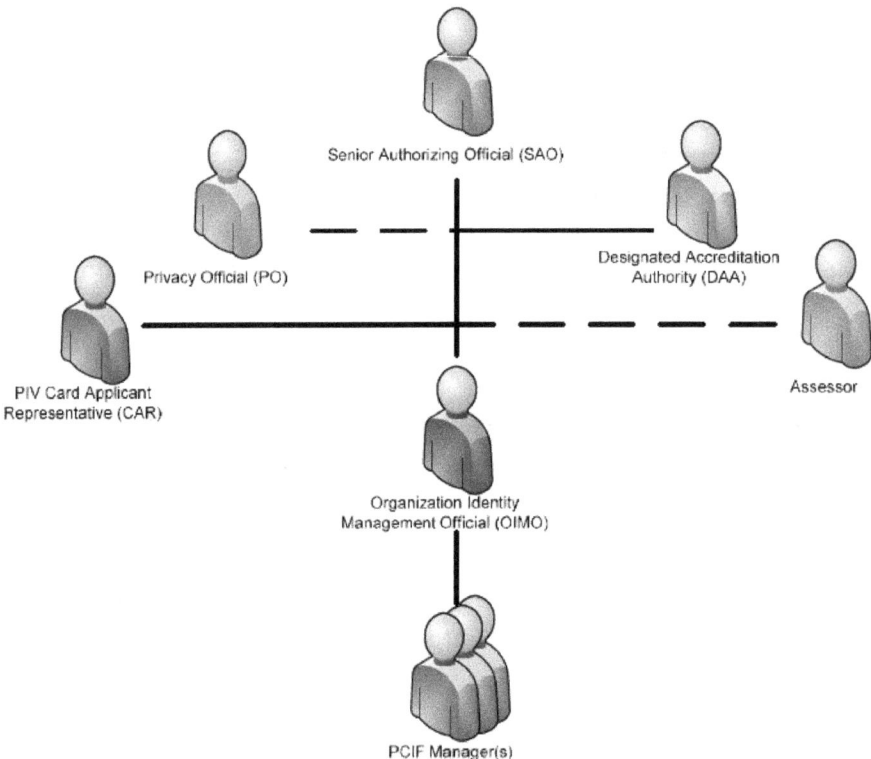

Figure 2 - PCI Accreditation Roles

2.7 The Relationship between SP 800-79-1 and SP 800-37

While accreditation is the major topic of both special publications, the goals of accreditation are distinct in SP 800-37 and SP 800-79-1. Accreditation under SP 800-37, as mandated by Appendix III of the Office of Management and Budget (OMB) Circular A-130, focuses on "authorizing processing" of information systems based on an assessment of security at the information system level. Accreditation as discussed herein and as mandated by HSPD-12 is concerned with the assessment of the "reliability" of a PCI to perform its functions in accordance with FIPS 201-1. An accreditation decision granted under SP 800-37 signifies that an organization official accepts responsibility for the security (in terms of confidentiality, integrity, and availability of information) of the information system. Accreditation of a PCI's reliability under SP 800-79-1 indicates that the organization official agrees to accept the risk that the PCI can operate within the control objectives outlined in HSPD-12 for "secure and reliable forms of identification." However in both cases, the organization official (Authorizing Official (AO) in the case of SP 800-37, and DAA in the case of SP 800-79-1) accepts responsibility, and is fully accountable for any adverse impacts to the organization if a breach in security, privacy, or policy occurs.

SP 800-79-1 focuses on the accreditation of an organization's capability and reliability, but depends on adequate security for all the supporting information systems that have been accredited under SP 800-37. Therefore, before the organization official accredits the PCI and its facilities, all PCI information systems used must be accredited.

In many cases, accreditation under SP 800-37 will be granted by an organization official different than the official responsible for accrediting the PCI. The former is an organization official tasked with making a decision on whether to authorize operation of an information system based on its security posture. The latter must be someone designated specifically for authorizing the operation of the PCI after it has been assessed and determined to be compliant with FIPS 201-1 control objectives.

2.8 Preparing for a PCI's Assessment

To facilitate an assessment of a PCI in a timely, efficient, and thorough manner, it is essential that all members of the Assessment team and staff of the PCI understand their specific roles and responsibilities, and participate as needed. The PCI, its facility personnel, and the team responsible for performing the assessment must cooperate and collaborate in a joint manner to ensure the success of the assessment. Specific responsibilities of the assessment team are listed below. For further information, including considerations that an organization may want to take into account when outsourcing assessments, refer to NIST Interagency Report (IR) 7328, *Security Assessment Provider Requirements and Customer Responsibilities: Building a Security Assessment Credentialing Program for Federal Information Systems*.

2.8.1 PCI Duties

Before the assessment can begin, an Assessor must be designated. The Assessor conducts the assessment and oversees the assessment team if one is needed. The assessment team may be made up of employees from the organization or personnel provided by a public or private sector entity contracted to provide services. Members of the assessment team should have various capabilities that are required to perform the activities specified in this document. Assessment team members should work together to prepare for, conduct, and document the findings of the PCI's assessment and assessments of all PCI facilities within the PCI boundary. Each team must be made up of individuals that collectively have the knowledge, skills, and abilities to conduct, evaluate, and document all assessments, including those performed on the information systems within the PCI.

Once an assessment team is in place, the OIMO and other relevant PCI personnel should begin the preparation for the assessment. Thorough preparations by both the PCI and the assessment team are important aspects of conducting an effective assessment. The PCI sets the stage for the assessment by identifying all appropriate personnel and making them available during the assessment. A fundamental requirement for accreditation is interviews by the assessment team of all PCI personnel. Personnel and officials must be notified of the pending assessment, must understand their roles in the process, and must be made available in accordance with the planned assessment schedule.

The OIMO must ensure that all relevant documentation has been completed and organized before the assessment begins. This documentation includes policies and procedures, organizational structure, information system architecture, product and vendor details, and specifics regarding the implementation of all the requirements from FIPS 201-1 and related publications. If the PCI has outsourced functions to an external service provider, all necessary documentation must be obtained from the provider regarding those operations utilized by the PCI. Before providing any documentation to the assessment team, the OIMO must review it to make certain it is both current and approved.

Another significant activity during the assessment is the observation by the assessment team of actual processes performed by the PCI. In order for the assessment team to confirm that processes are implemented in accordance with the operations plan, the PCI will need to ensure that assessment team members have access to, and are able to observe, PCI processes in real time. This could include scheduling enrollment/identity proofing, adjudication, card production, card activation/issuance, and maintenance activities for observation by the assessment team.

In order to aid the PCI's planning and preparation for the assessment, Appendix C includes a readiness review checklist. The checklist contains items needed during the assessment process. Satisfying this list of items before the assessment commences will facilitate efficient utilization of the assessment team's time, and will contribute towards the overall effectiveness of the assessment activity.

2.8.2 Assessment Team Duties

The independence of the assessment team is an important factor in assessing the credibility of the assessment results. In order to ensure that the results of the assessment are impartial and unbiased, the members of the assessment team must not be involved in the development, day-to-day maintenance, and operations of the PCI, or in the removal, correction, or remediation of deficiencies.

The assessment team may obtain information during an assessment that the organization does not want to disclose publicly. The assessment team has an obligation to safely and securely store and protect the confidentiality of all security assessment related records and information, including limiting access to the individuals that need to know the information. When using, storing, and transmitting information related to the PCI assessment, the assessment team shall follow the guidelines established by the organization in addition to all relevant laws, regulations, and standards regarding the need, protection, and privacy of information.

2.9 Accreditation Decisions

An accreditation decision is a judgment made by the DAA regarding authorizing operation of a PCI and its facilities. The DAA reviews the results of the assessment, considers the impact to the organization of any identified deficiencies, and then decides whether to authorize the operation of the PCI and its facilities. In doing so, the DAA is agreeing to accept the security and privacy risks to the organization in issuing and maintaining PIV Cards.

During the accreditation decision process, the DAA must evaluate the assessment findings for the PCI and each facility within the accreditation boundary. If the PCI has outsourced some of its services or functions, the DAA must review all relevant assessments and accreditations that have been granted to the external service provider and include them as a part of the overall evaluation of risk to the organization.

An authorization decision by a DAA must always be granted for a specific PCI before commencement of operations, and for each PCI there can be only one authorization decision. In issuing this decision, the DAA must indicate the PCI accreditation boundary to which the authorization applies. A DAA grants an authorization to a PCI, and then specifies which facilities (along with any exceptions or restrictions) are permitted to operate under that authorization. This allows the PCI and any authorized facilities to begin operations while any remaining facilities focus on addressing deficiencies with FIPS 201-1 and its supporting documents. At a later date, these latter facilities can be reassessed. After reviewing the new findings, the DAA can reissue the authorization for the PCI and expand the accreditation boundary to which the authorization applies by including the newly assessed facilities.

The major input to the accreditation decision is the assessment report. To ensure the assessment report is properly interpreted and the justification for the accreditation decision properly communicated, the DAA should meet with the Assessor, the OIMO, and the PCI Facility Manager(s) prior to issuing an accreditation decision to discuss the assessment findings and the terms and conditions of the authorization.

There are three accreditation alternatives that can be rendered by the DAA:

- Authorization to operate;
- Interim authorization to operate; or
- Denial of authorization to operate.

2.9.1 Authorization to Operate

If, after reviewing the results of the assessment phase, the DAA deems that the PCI and its facilities conform to FIPS 201-1 to an acceptable degree, and will continue to do so reliably during the accreditation validity period, an *authorization to operate* (ATO) may be issued. The PCI and its facilities are authorized to perform services in compliance with all relevant policies, in conformance to all relevant standards, and in accordance with the documented operations plan. The DAA shall indicate exactly which facilities are included in the ATO accreditation decision. An ATO can only be granted to a PCI if there are no limitations or restrictions imposed on any of its facilities that are included in the accreditation boundary.

After receiving an ATO under SP 800-79-1, re-accreditation shall be performed within three (3) years, or when there is a significant change in personnel or operating procedures (includes both improvement and degradation of operations) of a PCI, or when additional PCIFs are being added to a PCI. There may also be cases where one or more PCIFs cease operation. If this situation results in a PCI service identified in the PCI's Operations Plan becoming unavailable, then the

DAA must issue a Denial of Authorization to Operate (DATO- See Section 2.9.3). On the other hand On the other hand, if the PCI can continue to provide all services in the PCI's Operations Plan, then the accreditation decision letter has to be modified to exclude those facilities that have ceased operations (thus revising the accreditation boundary). The required PCI re-accreditation activities are at the discretion of the DAA and based on the extent and type of change.

2.9.2 Interim Authorization to Operate

If, after reviewing the results of the assessment phase, the DAA deems the discrepancies to be significant, but there is an overarching necessity to allow the PCI and its facilities to operate, an *interim authorization to operate (IATO)* may be issued. An interim authorization to operate is rendered when the identified deficiencies in the PCI and its facilities are significant, but can be addressed in a timely manner. These deficiencies must be documented so that they can be addressed during the planning of corrective actions. An interim authorization is an authorization to operate under specific terms and conditions. The DAA shall indicate exactly which facilities are included in the IATO accreditation decision during this interim period, along with any limitations or restrictions imposed. The maximum duration of an IATO is three (3) months. A maximum of two (2) consecutive IATOs may be granted for a PCI. Failure to correct deficiencies found in the PCI after the expiration of the second IATO must result in an issuance of a denial of authorization to operate (DATO) for the PCI. The accreditation boundary may be revised to exclude PCI Facilities that exhibit significant deficiencies in performing their functions.

A PCI is *not considered* accredited during the period of an IATO. When the deficiencies have been corrected, the IATO should be replaced with an ATO. Significant changes in the status of the PCI (e.g. addition of new facilities) that occur during the IATO period shall be reported immediately to the DAA.

2.9.3 Denial of Authorization to Operate

If, after reviewing the results of the assessment phase, the DAA deems operation of the PCI to be unacceptable, a *denial of authorization to operate (DATO)* shall be transmitted to the OIMO. Failure to receive authorization to operate indicates that there are major deficiencies in reliably meeting the requirements of FIPS 201-1 and its related documents. The PCI is not accredited and must not be allowed to operate. If the PCI is currently in operation, all functions must be halted including all operations in its facilities. If the PCI was previously accredited and had issued PIV Cards under an ATO, the OIMO along with the PCIF Manager(s) should consider whether a revocation of PIV Cards is necessary. The DAA and the Assessor should work with the OIMO and PCIF Manager(s) to ensure that proactive measures are taken to correct the deficiencies.

A PCI must not be authorized to operate if one or more of its critical information systems has not been accredited or is issued a DATO under SP 800-37. In the case where an IATO (under SP 800-37) has been issued for an information system within the PCI, the DAA may issue no greater than an IATO to the PCI. Once the SP 800-37 IATO is replaced with an SP 800-37 ATO, the DAA can issue a SP 800-79-1 ATO. If the SP 800-37 ATO expires for one or more of information systems during the course of operation of a PCI, the OIMO shall assess the criticality of the system for PCI operations and present the analysis to the DAA. The DAA then can exercise the following options:

- Specify a short time during which the information systems of the PCI must be re-accredited under SP 800-37 without changing the PCI's ATO status;
- Downgrade the current SP 800-79-1 ATO to an IATO; or
- If circumstances warrant, issue a SP 800-79-1 DATO and halt all PCI operations.

2.10 The Use of Risk in the Accreditation Decision

Accreditation is the official management decision by the DAA to authorize operation of a PCI, based on an assessment of its reliability and an acceptance of the risk inherent in that decision. By granting an authorization to operate, the DAA accepts responsibility for the reliability of the PCI and is fully accountable for any adverse impact to the organization or any other organization from cards issued by the PCI, its facilities, and any external service providers.

The assessment of a PCI provides the DAA with the basis for not only determining its reliability, but also for determining whether to accept the risk to the organization in granting an ATO. As the requirements in FIPS 201-1 and related documents form the basis of the assessment and are ultimately derived from the policy objectives of HSPD-12, those not reliably met by the PCI and its facilities represent the potential for adverse impact.

Implementation of an HSPD-12 program exposes an organization to specific risks at the mission level of the organization. The PIV Card is used to establish assurance of the identity of the cardholder, and as such, it must be trusted as a basis for granting access to the logical and physical resources of the organization. Any problem with an issued PIV Card that undermines that assurance could expose an organization to harm. Furthermore, the collection, processing, and dissemination of significant amounts of personal information required to issue a PIV Card increases the threat of this information being used for malicious purposes. It is the DAA's responsibility to weigh the risks of these and other security and privacy impacts of issuing PIV Cards when making the accreditation decision.

Furthermore, as HSPD-12 is a government-wide mandate based on a standard of interoperability allowing organizations to accept other organizations' PIV Cards, accreditation decisions within a single organization directly impact other organizations. For example, an interoperable identity credential issued by an accredited organization becomes the source of trust for another organization to authorize access to physical and logical resources, based on verification of that identity. The DAA's signature on the accreditation letter thus signifies his/her acceptance of responsibility (i.e., accountability) for the operations of the PCI, not only to the issuing organization, but also to other organizations that are in the federated circle of trust.

2.11 Accreditation Submission Package and Supporting Documentation

The *accreditation submission package* documents the results of the assessment phase and provides the DAA with the essential information needed to make a credible, risk-based decision on whether to authorize operation of the PCI. Unless specifically designated otherwise by the

DAA, the OIMO is responsible for the assembly, compilation, and submission of the accreditation package. The accreditation package contains the following documents:

- The PCI operations plan (including all PCI Facilities Standard Operating Procedures [SOPs] and attachments)
- SP 800-37 accreditation letters
- The assessment report
- The corrective actions plan (if required)

The PCI operations plan contains the PCI's policies, procedures, and processes for all the major PCI functional areas. The operations plan provides a complete picture of the structure, management, and operations of the PCI to the Assessor and DAA. Appendix D provides a template of what to include in the PCI operations plan. One of the most significant pieces of information contained within the operations plan is the list of PCI controls, how they were implemented, and who is responsible for their management. This description of the PCI controls makes it a simple process for the Assessor to quickly ascertain how they were implemented and by whom.

If certain functions described in the operations plan are outsourced, the PCI's operation plan can reference or "point to" the external service provider's operation plan and related documentation, such as support agreements and any contracts. In this manner, the Assessor has access to the information regarding the external service provider's operations without requiring the PCI to duplicate any documentation.

The SP 800-37 accreditation letters are the formal authorization to operate the PCI information systems that are directly involved in the issuance and maintenance of PIV Cards.

The PCI assessment report, prepared by the Assessor, provides the information needed to determine the extent to which the requirements are being met and are expected to continue as such during future operations. For each deficiency that is found, the assessment report must include the potential impact of the deficiency if it continues without correction and the recommended corrective action to correct it. Appendix E provides a template of what to include in the assessment report.

The corrective actions plan (CAP), prepared by the OIMO with the assistance of the Assessor, describes the changes needed to correct deficiencies noted during the assessment with a time frame for completing each change.

The OIMO submits the accreditation submission package to the DAA.[2] Figure 3 illustrates the primary components of the accreditation submission package.

---

[2] Accreditation packages may be submitted in either paper or electronic format. Appropriate measures should be employed to protect the information contained in accreditation packages (electronic or paper format) in accordance with organization policy.

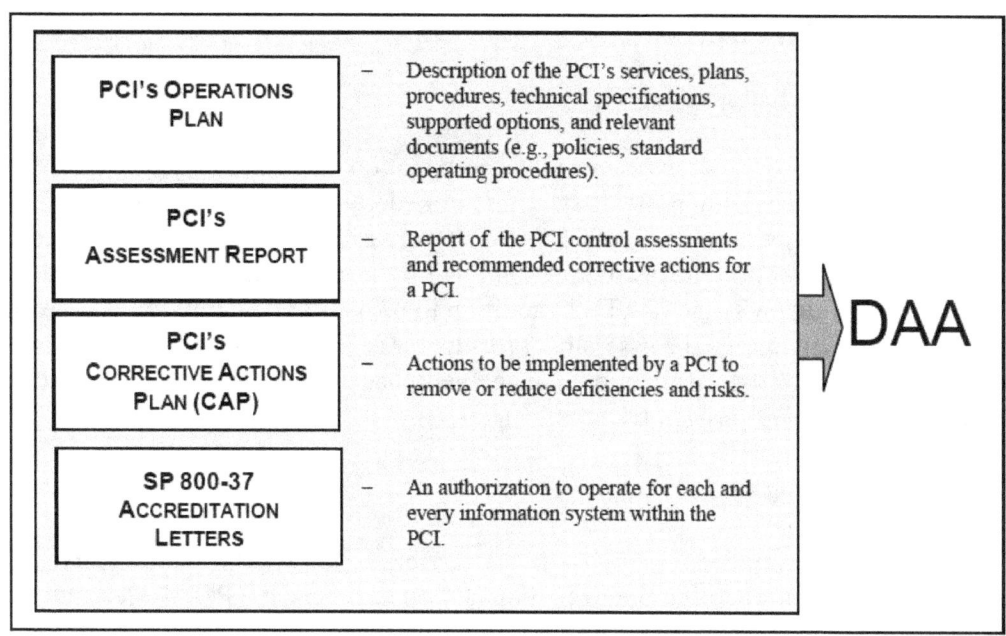

Figure 3 - Accreditation Submission Package

Upon receiving and reviewing the accreditation package and in consultation with the Assessor, the DAA decides whether to authorize operations of the PCI. The accreditation decision letter transmits the accreditation decision from the DAA to the OIMO. The accreditation decision letter contains the following information:

- Accreditation decision;
- Supporting rationale for the decision; and
- Terms and conditions for the authorization, including which PCIFs are included.

The accreditation decision letter (see Appendix F for examples) informs the OIMO that the PCI is— (i) authorized to operate; (ii) authorized to operate on an interim basis; or (iii) not authorized to operate. The supporting rationale includes the justification for the DAA's decision. The terms and conditions for the authorization provide a description of any limitations or restrictions placed on the operation of the PCI, including which PCIFs are included in the decision. The accreditation decision letter is attached to the original accreditation submission package and becomes the accreditation decision package.

The DAA sends the accreditation decision package to the OIMO and retains a copy of it. The OIMO carefully reviews the terms and conditions of authorization before initiating the necessary steps for PCI operations. Both parties mark the accreditation decision package appropriately for storage under the organization's retention policy.

3. PIV CARD ISSUER (PCI) COMPLIANCE

3.1 Introducing PCI Controls

Accreditation of a PCI is a broader endeavor than accreditation of the security of an information system under SP 800-37. The requirements specified in Federal Information Processing Standard (FIPS) 201-1 cover all major aspects of a PCI, including organizational preparedness; security management and data protection; infrastructure; and PCI processes. Each broad area is defined herein as a PCI Accreditation Topic (PAT). In addition to providing structure to the assessment, PATs are also used to summarize the assessment results for reporting. In addition, they are used to structure the report to senior organization management that provides an analysis of the strengths and weaknesses within the PCI.

The PCI Accreditation Topics:

- **Organizational Preparedness** relates to the capability, knowledge, and understanding of senior management regarding the formation and operation of the PCI. Roles and responsibilities must be clearly identified, and policies and procedures must be defined, documented, implemented, and enforced.

- **Security Management & Data Protection** involves implementing and operating appropriate security management procedures, operational controls, and technical protection measures to ensure that privacy requirements are satisfied, the rights of individuals are assured, and personal data is protected.

- **Infrastructure Elements** represents the activities required to procure, deploy, and maintain the PCI information system components. PCI information system components (e.g., PKI, biometrics, and card production) must meet the technical specifications defined in FIPS 201-1 and related documents. Additionally, information systems used within the PCI need to be certified and accredited under Special Publication (SP) 800-37 for FISMA compliance.

- **Processes** are classes of functions that collectively span the entire PIV lifecycle activities, such as sponsorship, enrollment/identity proofing, adjudication, card production, card activation/issuance, and maintenance.

Each PAT is sub-divided into one or more Accreditation Focus Areas. Each focus area is a set of closely-related requirements that need to be met by the PCI and its facilities. Each requirement and the procedure, process, or technical product (termed a "PCI control") used to satisfy each requirement listed under a focus area needs to be satisfied by a PCI. However, the manner in which the requirement is satisfied and how its specifications are implemented and managed may vary from organization to organization.

For instance, each PCI is required to identity-proof their applicants (i.e., use due diligence in validating the claimed identity of the applicant, using all documents provided by the applicant) prior to enrollment. This process can be implemented in one of several ways, depending upon the structure, size, and geographical distribution of an organization's facilities. The process could be conducted at a central location or could be distributed throughout the country within regional centers. It could be operated directly by the organization or by an outside service provider. However, irrespective of the implementation approach, this enrollment/identity-proofing activity needs to be reliably and accurately performed.

PCI controls are designed to satisfy specific requirements in FIPS 201-1 and its related documents. If the underlying specification requirements are mandatory, then the corresponding PCI controls are mandatory as well. There are also PCI controls associated with optional requirements in FIPS 201-1. This category of PCI controls also becomes mandatory if the PCI is implementing those optional requirements. An example is an optional requirement to store the electronic facial image of the card holder in the PIV Card. If the PCI's card activation/issuance's process implements this option, then the associated PCI control should be assessed with an acceptable result.

The evidence that ensures the presence of PCI controls that are derived from FIPS 201-1 requirements and its related documents as well as OMB Memoranda, and verified through appropriate assessments, establishes the <u>capability</u> of a PCI. However, accreditation is generally based not merely on the demonstration of capability, but also on the presence of certain organizational characteristics that will provide a high degree of confidence to the Assessor that the demonstrated capabilities will be carried out in a dependable and sustainable manner. This dependability measure, or <u>reliability</u> (as it is generally called), has to be established by adequately assessing that a PCI has the desired organizational characteristics, including adequate facilities, appropriate equipment, trained personnel, adequate resources, trustworthy management, and properly vetted operations staff. Hence, the accreditation methodology includes a set of PCI controls, verification of which establishes the reliability of a PCI. This set of controls is grouped under the accreditation focus area "Facility and Personnel Readiness". These reliability-relevant PCI controls are formulated, based on "commonly accepted security readiness measures" that have evolved in response to lessons learned in security incidents that have taken place due to threats, such as insider attacks, and risks, such as physical security lapses. In addition to the controls provided herein, an organization may develop additional mission-specific controls that will contribute towards the overall reliability of the PCI to meet the organization's mission needs.

Table 1 provides a listing of the four PIV Accreditation Topics (PATs) and the Accreditation Focus Areas under each topic:

Organizational Preparedness
Preparation and Maintenance of Documentation (DO)
Assignment of Roles and Responsibilities (RR)
Facility and Personnel Readiness (FP)
Security Management & Data Protection
Protection of Stored and Transmitted Data (ST)
Enforcement of Applicable Privacy Requirements (PR)
Infrastructure Elements
Deployed Products & Information Systems (DP)

Implementation of Credential Infrastructures (CI)
Processes
Sponsorship Process (SP)
Enrollment/Identity-Proofing Process (EI)
Adjudication Process (AP)
Card Production Process (CP)
Card Activation/Issuance Process (AI)
Maintenance Process (MP)

Table 1 - PATs and Associated Accreditation Focus Areas

Appendix G contains required PCI controls grouped by PAT and Accreditation Focus Area. Each PCI control represents how one or more requirements from FIPS 201-1 and its related documents can be satisfied. PCI controls are sequentially numbered using the two-character identifier assigned to the Accreditation Focus Area under which they are listed. Table 2 shows the relationships between PATs, Accreditation Focus Areas, and PCI controls.

	PAT = Organizational Preparedness		
Accreditation Focus Area	**Identifier**	**PCI Control**	**Source**
Preparation and Maintenance of Documentation (DO)	DO-1	The organization develops and implements a PCI operations plan according to the template in Appendix D. The operations plan references other documents as needed.	SP 800-79-1, Section 2.11 – Accreditation Package and Supporting Documentation
	DO-2	The organization has a written policy and procedures for enrollment/identity proofing that has been approved by the head of the organization.	FIPS 201-1, Section 2.2– PIV Identity Proofing and Registration Requirements

Table 2 - PAT, Accreditation Focus Area, and PCI Control Relationships

Irrespective of whether the information systems utilized within the PCI and its facilities are categorized at low, moderate, or high impact levels according to FIPS 199, the same set of PCI controls apply, regardless of an individual system's impact level. Furthermore, nothing precludes a PCI from implementing additional controls to ensure a higher level of confidence in mitigating risks associated with issuing PIV Cards.

3.2 Implementing PCI Controls

Each PCI control must be properly implemented, managed, and monitored in order for the PCI to be accredited. Depending on how an organization decides to implement their HSPD-12 program, the authority to implement some of the controls may not directly come under the PCI Management (due to outsourcing of certain PCI processes or using the PCI facilities of other organizations). However, it is still the responsibility of the PCI management to ensure that these PCI controls are being deployed, enforced, and maintained by its service provider.

3.2.1 PCI Controls implemented at the Organization or Facility Level

The nature of each PCI control dictates where it is implemented. Controls that are common to or impact multiple PCI processes are implemented at the organization level. The development of the PCI operations plan is an example of a PCI control implemented at the organizational level. Generally, controls specific to a process are implemented at the facility where that process or function is carried out. For example, the control that states that a "1:1 biometric match of the applicant against the biometric included in the PIV Card or in the PIV enrollment record must be performed before releasing the PIV Card to the applicant" is implemented at a card activation/issuance facility.

4. ASSESSMENTS

An assessment is a set of activities performed by the Assessor to gain assurance that the PIV Card Issuer (PCI) controls have been implemented properly and meet their required function or purpose. Understanding the overall effectiveness of the PCI controls implemented in the PCI and its facilities is essential in determining the risk to the organization's overall mission, and forms the basis for the accreditation decision by the Designated Accreditation Authority (DAA).

An Assessor must– (i) compile evidence that the PCI controls employed in the PCI are implemented correctly, operating as intended, and producing the desired results; and (ii) present this evidence in a manner such that the DAA can make a credible, risk-based decision about the operation of the PCI.

The focus of an assessment is the PCI controls, each of which is designed to satisfy one or more specific requirements from FIPS 201-1 and related documents. The objective for the Assessor is to use the assessment procedures associated with each PCI control (described in Appendix G) as a means to measure if the PCI being assessed meets the requirements. The assessment procedures are designed to facilitate the gathering of evidence that PCI controls are implemented correctly, operating as intended, and producing the desired outcome.

In preparation for a PCI assessment, the Assessor performs the following two preparatory steps:

- Determination of the accreditation boundary to understand the target of the assessment. The accreditation boundary dictates which PCIFs and outsourced services are to be included in the assessment.

- Review of the PCI operations plan to determine which PCI controls are implemented at the organizational level and which at the facility level. This analysis should provide the Assessor with an understanding of where different responsibilities lie within the PCI and how to address them during the assessment.

In cases where a PCI has outsourced functions, the PCI is responsible for ensuring that the external service provider has implemented the control. During the assessment, it is the service provider's responsibility to provide documentation to the Assessor regarding the implementation of that control. If results from a previous assessment of the service provider (provided the current assessment is part of re-accreditation after substantial changes) can be referenced, the Assessor may elect to incorporate these results (not exceeding one year) or re-do part or all of the assessment. The extent of re-use of the results of the previous assessment is entirely at the discretion of the Assessor.

PCI controls implemented at the organizational level generally need to be assessed only once, since these controls span across the entire PCI and its facilities. In other words, these controls may not be re-assessed when the accreditation boundary changes (e.g., due to addition of facilities). Examples of organizational level controls include the set of controls under the accreditation focus areas Preparation and Maintenance of Documentation (DO) and Assignment of Roles and Responsibilities (RR).

There are certain controls that although they are put in place at the organizational level, they need to be reviewed at the PCIF level. An example of such a control artifact is "contingency/disaster recovery plan for information systems". Though the development of the contingency/disaster recovery plan is an organizational level control, a review of this control artifact is needed whenever new information systems in the existing facilities or new facilities are added to ensure that these new systems are brought within the scope of the plan.

Unlike organization level PCI controls, facility level PCI controls need to be assessed individually at each facility. A facility is often designated based on the type of PCI process it performs (exceptions are the Sponsorship Process and Adjudication Process). Hence, for example, if there are multiple facilities for enrollment/identify proofing (e.g., multiple enrollment centers), assessment of the PCI controls under the focus area Enrollment/Identity Proofing should take place in each of the enrollment centers. However, if all facilities are operating using uniform operational procedures and underlying information systems, it is acceptable to perform assessments at facilities that are selected randomly or through some other established criteria (e.g., geographical region or service provider).

Prior assessments may be used as a starting point for the assessment of a PCI. While past assessments provide insight into the implementation and operation of the PCI, a number of factors affect the validity of past assessments. These include updates in policies and procedures, changes in systems/technology, and turnover in employees and contractors. Any significant changes in one or more of these factors should trigger a new assessment of the PCI. The Assessor must validate whether a PCI is currently operating as expected using the given assessment procedures, including specially tailored or augmented procedures. It is only through a current valid assessment of PCI controls that the Assessor and Organization Identity Management Official (OIMO) will have confidence in the reliability of the PCI and its facilities.

The use of automated security controls, if reliably implemented and maintained in information systems, results in a high assurance of the protection of information and other organizational assets. Human involvement results in more variability in how PCI controls are implemented and operated, as security and reliability depend on many factors, including an individual's training, knowledge, motivation, experience, and management. Relying on humans for data protection, rather than on reliable, automated security mechanisms, makes it critical that trust and reliability assessments of management, operators, and maintenance personnel are current and up-to-date. Many of the assessment procedures rely on interactions among the Assessor, PCI management, and facilities staff. Interviews with all involved personnel and observations of all PCI processes are required. On-site visits, real-time observations, and reviews of processes are essential, as the Assessor must not rely solely on documentation to determine if a given PCI control has been implemented.

4.1 Assessment Methods

One or more assessment procedures are associated with each PCI control listed in Appendix G. An assessment procedure is carried out using one or more of the following assessment methods. (The assessment methods associated with an assessment procedure are given in parenthesis in Appendix G)

- *Review* – An evaluation of documentation that describes plans, policies, and procedures in order to verify that they are adequate, understood by the PCI management and operations personnel, and that they are in accordance with applicable policies, regulations, standards, technical guidelines, and organizational guidance.
- *Interview* – a directed conversation with one or more PCI personnel in which both pre-established and follow-on questions are asked, responses documented, discussion encouraged, and conclusions reached.
- *Observe* – a real-time viewing of PCI processes in operation, including all information system components of the PCI involved in creation, issuance, maintenance, and replacement of PIV Cards.
- *Test* – an evaluation of a component against a set of relevant PIV specifications using applicable test methods and metrics (as given in the associated assessment procedure in Appendix G).

These methods are intended to provide the Assessor with sufficient, precise, accurate, and relevant evidence regarding an accreditation topic and focus area. One or more assessment methods may be required to determine if the PCI has satisfactorily met the objective outlined for that assessment procedure. Assessment results are used by the Assessor to determine the overall effectiveness of the PCI control.

Table 3 shows an example of the relationships among a PAT, an Accreditation Focus Area, several PCI controls, and their assessment procedures.

\multicolumn{4}{c}{**PAT = Organizational Preparedness**}			
Accreditation Focus Area	**Identifier**	**PCI Control**	**Source**
Preparation and Maintenance of Documentation	DO-1	The organization develops and implements a PCI operations plan according to the template in Appendix D. The operations plan references other documents as needed. **Assessment** *Determine that:* (i.) *the operations plan includes the relevant elements from the template in Appendix D (review);* (ii.) *the operations plan includes the list of PCI controls and included with each is the PCI control owner, how they were implemented and whether they are organization or facility specific (review);* (iii.) *documentation that is not included in the operations plan is referenced accurately (review);* (iv.) *the operations plan is reviewed and approved by the DAA within the organization (review, interview).*	SP 800-79-1, Section 2.11 – Accreditation Package and Supporting Documentation

		DO-2	The organization has written policies and procedures for enrollment/identity proofing that are approved by the head of the organization. **Assessment** *Determine that*: (i) *the organization has developed and documented written policy and procedures for identity proofing and enrollment for personnel requiring a PIV Card (e.g. employees, contractors and foreign nationals) (review);* (ii) *the policy is consistent with the organization's mission and functions, FIPS 201-1 and applicable laws, directives, policies, regulations, standards, and guidance (review);* (iii) *the policy and procedures have been signed off by the head of the organization (review);* (iv) *the organization will periodically review and update the policy and procedures as required (review, interview).*	FIPS 201-1, Section 2.2– PIV Identity Proofing and Registration Requirements

Table 3 - Sample PCI Controls with Assessment Procedures

Some organizations may need to customize some of the PCI controls to meet their specific characteristics and mission needs. In such cases, the associated assessment procedures may also have to be customized/augmented to ensure proper implementation of these controls.

4.2 The Assessment Report

The Assessment report contains the results of the assessment in a format that facilitates reviewing by the DAA. The DAA must evaluate the information in the Assessment report in order to make a sound, credible decision regarding the residual risk of authorizing the operations of the PCI.

An Assessment report template is provided in Appendix E. The report is organized by Accreditation Focus Area. For each PCI control, it must be documented as to which entity is responsible for the implementation of that control (the organization or an external service provider) and if the PCI control is at the organizational or facility level.

> **Card Activation/Issuance Process**
>
> PCI Control Identifier— AI-7
>
> PCI Control Description— The issuer performs a 1:1 biometric match of the applicant against the biometric included in the PIV Card or in the enrollment record. On successful match, the PIV Card shall be released to the applicant
>
> PCI Control Owner/ Control Level — External Service Provider/Facility Level
>
> Assessment Result— Partially Satisfied
>
> Assessment Findings— There is operational evidence that a 1:1 biometric match is carried out before the card is released to the applicant.
>
> Assessment Deficiency and Potential Impact— The requirement to carry out this task is not documented clearly enough in the operations plan. Although personnel are knowledgeable about this requirement, and the task was observed to be performed correctly during card issuance, the lack of documentation could be a problem if there is turnover in staff.
>
> Recommendation— Update the issuance process description within the operations plan to include a clear description of this task in the process.

Figure 4 - Sample Assessment Report

The assessment result associated with each PCI control shall be one of the following:
- Satisfied
- Partially Satisfied
- Not Satisfied
- Not Applicable

After carrying out an assessment procedure, the Assessor records his/her conclusion in one of two ways: MET, NOT MET. Using the list of conclusions pertaining to assessment procedures associated with a PCI control, the assessment result (which is one of the 4 outcomes listed above) is arrived at as follows:

- If the conclusion from all assessment procedures is MET, then the assessment result for the PCI control is "Satisfied"

- If some of the conclusions are NOT MET, then the assessment result for the PCI control is marked as either "Partially Satisfied" or "Not Satisfied", depending on whether or not any of the underlying tasks in the assessment procedures are critical (i.e., they represent the only way to meet the PCI control's objective). An example of an assessment that resulted in "Partially Satisfied" is given in Figure 4. In this instance, there is an awareness of a task requirement, and the task itself is being carried out, but the reference to the task is missing in the document.

In drawing a conclusion after carrying out an assessment procedure, the Assessor must consider the potential subjective and objective aspects of the assessment methods used (e.g., interviews, document reviews, observations, and tests) for that assessment procedure. Deficiencies that result in "Partially Satisfied" or "Not Satisfied" must be reported by the Assessor. The Assessor must also outline the potential adverse impacts if the PCI control is deployed with the identified deficiencies.

The assessment report template provides the means for recording the assessment result for each PCI control. The assessment results for all PCI controls are aggregated to generate the assessment report for a PCI accreditation focus area. The set of PCI Accreditation Focus Area Reports is aggregated to generate a PCI accreditation topic report. Finally, the group of PCI Accreditation Topic Reports is used to generate the overall PCI Assessment Report and an accompanying Executive Summary (intended for Senior Management).

5.0 ACCREDITATION

The accreditation of a PIV Card Issuer (PCI) consists of four phases: (i) Initiation; (ii) Assessment; (iii) Accreditation; and (iv) Monitoring. Each phase consists of tasks and sub-tasks that are to be carried out by the responsible officials (e.g., the Designated Accreditation Authority (DAA), Assessor, Organization Identity Management Official (OIMO), and PCI Facility (PCIF) Manager(s)). Figure 5 provides a view of the accreditation phases, including the tasks associated with each phase. A table of accreditation phases, tasks, sub-tasks, and the official responsible for each is provided in Appendix H.

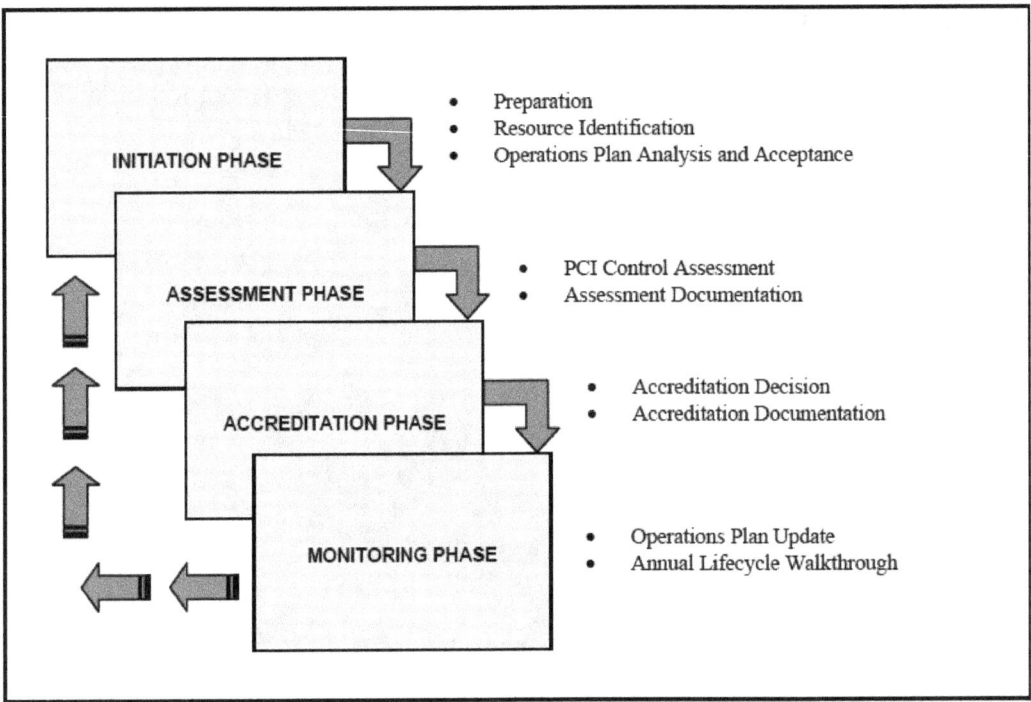

Figure 5 - Accreditation Phases

5.1 Initiation Phase

The Initiation Phase consists of three tasks: (i) preparation; (ii) resource identification; and (iii) operations plan analysis and acceptance. The primary purpose of this phase is to ensure that the PCI is prepared for the assessment, including having all the resources and documentation in place. The other purpose of this phase is to include the DAA early in the process in order to assure success of the assessment and accreditation.

Task 1: Preparation

The objectives of this task are to prepare for accreditation by reviewing the PCI operations plan and confirming that the plan is consistent with Federal Information Processing Standard (FIPS) 201-1 and the template provided herein.

> **Subtask 1.1:** Confirm that the PCI and its operations have been fully described and documented in the PCI's operations plan.

Responsibility: OIMO

Guidance: The PCI operation plan includes, at a minimum, the sections defined in the operations plan template in Appendix D. It is the OIMO's responsibility to ensure that the organization's PCI operations plan incorporates a complete and accurate description of the PCI's operations. If a process or function is provided by an external service provider, their operating procedures should be documented and incorporated by reference in the PCI operations plan. In this case, the operations plan includes a pointer, guiding the reader to additional documentation and information.

Subtask 1.2: Confirm that processes followed at the PCI Facility are conducted in accordance with the policies and procedures specified in the PCI operations plan and are documented in standard operating procedures.

Responsibility: OIMO, PCIF Manager

Guidance: Even though PCI Facilities may be following requirements from FIPS 201-1, their processes need to be consistent with those prescribed by the PCI's operations plan and documented in standard operating procedures.

Task 2: Resource Identification

The objectives of the resource identification task are to– (i) identify and document the resources required for assisting with the assessment; (ii) identify the scope of the assessment and accreditation boundary; and (ii) prepare a plan of assessment activities indicating the proposed schedule and key milestones.

Subtask 2.1: Identify the Senior Authorizing Official (SAO), Designated Accreditation Authority (DAA), Privacy Official (PO), PCIF Managers, Assessor, and other key personnel at the facility level who are performing functions, such as enrollment/identity proofing, card production, and card activation/issuance. Maintenance personnel also should be contacted to provide requested assessment information to the Assessor.

Responsibility: OIMO

Guidance: Notify these individuals of the upcoming assessment, and inform them of the need for their participation during the process.

Subtask 2.2: Determine the accreditation boundary for the PCI.

Responsibility: OIMO; DAA

Guidance: The accreditation boundary determines the target of the assessment. In preparation for a PCI assessment, the OIMO and DAA should identify which PCIFs and external service providers are to be included. This ensures that functions performed and processes managed by the external service provider are considered during the accreditation process. An organization may want to include only those PCIFs that are ready to operate; other facilities can be assessed at a later date.

Subtask 2.3: Determine the resources and the time needed for the accreditation of the PCI, and prepare a plan for execution of the assessment.

Responsibility: OIMO; DAA

Guidance: The level of effort required for an assessment depends on numerous factors— (i) the size the PCI; (ii) the location and number of its facilities; (iii) the level of outsourcing utilized by the PCI; and (iv) the number of cards being, or to be issued. By examining factors that could influence the complexity of the assessment, the organization can make informed judgments about the size of the assessment team, the resources needed to support the assessment, and the time-frame for completing it.

Task 3: Operations Plan Analysis and Acceptance

The objectives of the operations plan analysis and acceptance task are: (i) determine if the requirements of FIPS 201-1 have been implemented; (ii) evaluate the PCI operations plan and revise as needed; and (iii) obtain acceptance of the plan by the DAA prior to conducting an assessment of the PCI controls.

Subtask 3.1: Review the list of required PCI controls documented in the organization's PCI operation plan and then confirm that they have been implemented properly.

Responsibility: DAA; OIMO

Guidance: Since the PCI controls serve as the basis for the assessment, review the PCI's documentation and operations plan to identify the controls that must be implemented before investing time in assessment activities such as interviews or testing. The operations plan must document each PCI control, whether it is organization or facility specific, the owner of the PCI control, and how the PCI control is implemented.

Subtask 3.2: Analyze the PCI operations plan to determine if there are deficiencies in satisfying all the policies, procedures, and other requirements in FIPS 201-1 that could result in a Denial of Authorization to Operate (DATO) being issued. After discussing the discovered deficiencies in the documentation and operations plan with the OIMO, the organization may still want to continue with the assessment, if it has determined that it can address all deficiencies within the time period of the current assessment. In this situation, the DAA can either authorize continuation of the assessment or terminate the assessment effort depending upon the evaluation of the PCI's ability to address the deficiencies.

Responsibility: DAA, OIMO

Guidance: The operations plan should adequately specify the policies, procedures, and processes of the PCI so that, subsequent to an initial review, deficiencies that could lead to an eventual DATO may be identified for the PCI.

Subtask 3.3: Verify that the PCI operations plan is acceptable.

Responsibility: DAA

Guidance: If the PCI operations plan is deemed acceptable, the DAA should authorize the accreditation processes to advance to the next phase. Acceptance of the PCI operations plan signifies that the resources required to initiate and complete the accreditation activities may be deployed.

5.2 Assessment Phase

The Assessment Phase consists of two tasks— (i) PCI control assessment; and (ii) assessment documentation. The purpose of this phase is to determine the extent to which the requirements of FIPS 201-1 are implemented correctly, operating as intended, and producing the desired outcomes. This phase also specifies actions to be taken to correct all identified deficiencies. An analysis of the impact of identified deficiencies that cannot be corrected or mitigated efficiently on the reliable operation of the PCI should be conducted and documented. Successful completion of this phase should provide the DAA with the information needed to make an appropriate accreditation decision.

Task 4: PCI Control Assessment

The objectives of this task are to— (i) initiate and conduct an assessment of the PCI controls; and (ii) document the results of the assessment. The Assessor shall first verify the acceptability of all documentation, including the operations plan and previous assessments, along with all relevant Federal laws, regulations, standards, and directives. PCI control assessment should then commence. The Assessor should schedule interviews, schedule real-time observations of PCI processes, and initiate all needed testing of the PIV Card and PCI information system components. Once the Assessor has gathered the results of the assessment procedures, descriptions of all discovered deficiencies shall be prepared, along with recommendations for removing these deficiencies.

Subtask 4.1: Review the suggested and selected assessment methods for each PCI control in preparation for the assessment.

Responsibility: Assessor

Guidance: Based on the accreditation boundary, the scope of the assessment should be established. The Assessor should review the selected assessment procedures (based on the scope of the assessment) in order to plan and coordinate activities for the assessment. For instance, if a particular PCI control requires the observation of a particular process, the Assessor will need to schedule this activity in a timely fashion after coordinating it with the PCI's or PCIF's management. The Assessor, as directed by the DAA, may supplement the assessment methods and procedures recommended in these guidelines. Assessment methods and procedures may be created or tailored for a particular PCI.

Subtask 4.2: Assemble all documentation and supporting materials necessary for the assessment of the PCI; if these documents include previous assessments, review the findings and determine if they are applicable to the current assessment.

Responsibility: OIMO; Assessor

Guidance: The OIMO assists the Assessor in gathering all relevant documents and supporting materials from the organization that will be required during the assessment of the PCI. Central to this effort is the PCI operations plan. The PCI's operations shall be completely described in the operations plan. The PCI operations plan may include by reference, or point to, the supporting materials. In this case, the OIMO will also need to gather this supporting material for the Assessor. Examples of other documentation include: (i) letters of appointment; (ii) privacy-related documentation; (iii) information forms utilized within the PCI; (iv) documentation from each outsourced service provider, including control implementation specifics, support and service level agreements, and contracts; (v) standard operating procedures for the PCIFs within the accreditation boundary for the PCI; and (vi) signed accreditation letters under SP 800-37 for all information systems within the PCI.

When previous assessments exist, including the one on which the current Authorization to Operate (ATO) is based, the Assessor is strongly encouraged to review these results. The Assessor may satisfy some of the PCI control assessment requirements by reviewing and referencing previous assessment report(s). Although previous assessments cannot be used as a substitute for the current assessment, they provide a snapshot view of the PCI and highlight problems that may have existed in the past.

Subtask 4.3: Assess the required PCI controls using the prescribed assessment procedures found in Appendix G.

Responsibility: Assessor

Guidance: The Assessor performs the assessment procedures selected for each PCI control to assess if the PCI controls have been implemented correctly, are operating as intended, and producing the desired outcomes. The Assessor uses the assessment methods specified in Section 4.1. Documentation collected in the previous task is reviewed, and any deficiencies are identified. Interviews can be used as an opportunity to clarify issues encountered during a review of the PCI documentation, as well as to determine the expertise of the personnel performing key functions with the PCI and its facilities. Processes need to be observed to ensure that they are being followed as documented and tests executed to determine if the PIV components have been configured and are operating in a PIV-compliant manner.

If the PCI and its facilities are being assessed, all the PCI controls will need to be assessed. If PIV services have been outsourced to an external provider, the Assessor shall verify that the PCI controls applying to those services have been assessed, and the reliability of the service provider has been found satisfactory. If a PCI and its facilities have already been assessed and are operating under a current ATO, and the purpose of the assessment is to add a facility(s) to the accreditation letter, the Assessor may reuse the results of a previous assessment for the organization level PCI controls and then assess a random sample of PCIFs.

Subtask 4.4: Prepare the assessment report.

Responsibility: Assessor

Guidance: The assessment report contains— (i) the results of the assessment; (ii) recommendations for correcting deficiencies; and (iii) the residual risk to the organization if those deficiencies are not corrected or mitigated. The assessment report is the Assessor's statement of the results of analyzing and evaluating the PCI's implementation of controls. The sample assessment report template in Appendix E should be used as a format for documenting the results after assessing the PCI controls.

Task 5: Assessment Documentation

This task consists of the Assessor submitting the assessment report to the OIMO and the latter adding the PCI operations plan (revised if necessary) and the corrective actions plan (CAP) to generate an accreditation submission package for the DAA. In situations where the assessment report contains deficiencies, the OIMO may choose to address some deficiencies based on the recommendations by the Assessor and revise the PCI operations plan (if needed), even before submitting the package for accreditation.

Subtask 5.1: Provide the OIMO with the assessment report.

Responsibility: Assessor

Guidance: The OIMO relies on the expertise, experience, and judgment of the Assessor to: (i) provide recommendations on how to correct deficiencies in the planned or performed operations; and (ii) to understand the potential impacts of those deficiencies. The OIMO may choose to act on selected recommendations of the Assessor before the accreditation package is finalized. To optimize the utilization of resources organization-wide, any actions taken by the OIMO prior to the final accreditation decision must be coordinated with the DAA. The Assessor reviews any changes made in response to the corrective actions and revises the assessment report, as appropriate.

Subtask 5.2: Revise the PCI operations plan (if necessary) and implement its new provisions.

Responsibility: OIMO

Guidance: The revised PCI operations plan must include all changes made in response to recommendations for corrective actions from the Assessor.

Subtask 5.3: Prepare the corrective actions plan (CAP).

Responsibility: OIMO

Guidance: The CAP, one of the three primary documents in the accreditation submission package, describes actions that must be taken by the OIMO to correct deficiencies identified in the Assessment phase. The CAP identifies— (i) the tasks to be accomplished; (ii) the resources required to accomplish the tasks; (iii) scheduled completion dates for the tasks, and (iv) the person designated as responsible for completing each of the tasks.

Subtask 5.4: Assemble the accreditation submission package and submit to the DAA.

Responsibility: OIMO

Guidance: The OIMO is responsible for the assembly and compilation of the accreditation submission package with inputs from the OIMO. The accreditation submission package shall contain: (i) the final assessment report; (ii) the CAP; (iii) the revised PCI operations plan; and (iv) the SP 800-37 accreditation letters for all information systems within the PCI. The OIMO may wish to consult other key organization participants (e.g., the Assessor, PO) prior to submitting the accreditation submission package to the DAA. The accreditation submission package can be submitted in either paper or electronic form. The contents of the accreditation submission package must be protected in accordance with organization policy.

5.3 Accreditation Phase

The Accreditation Phase consists of two tasks— (i) making an appropriate accreditation decision; and (ii) completing the accreditation documentation. Upon completion of this phase, the OIMO will have— (i) an authorization to operate the PCI services as defined in its operations plan; (ii) an interim authorization to operate under specific terms and conditions; or (iii) a denial of authorization to operate.

Task 6: Accreditation Decision

The accreditation decision task determines if the assessment phase has been satisfactorily completed so that a recommendation concerning the operation of the PCI can be made with assurance. The DAA, working with the Assessor, reviews the contents of the assessment submission package, the identified and uncorrected or un-correctable deficiencies, the potential impacts on each organization using the PCI's services, and the CAP in determining the final risk to the organization(s) and the acceptability of that risk in light of the organization's mission.

> **Subtask 6.1:** Review the assessment decision package to see if it is complete and that all applicable PCI controls have been fully assessed using the designated assessment procedures.
>
> **Responsibility:** DAA
>
> **Guidance:** Coverage for all PCI controls and proper adherence to assessment procedures and appropriate assessment methods helps to create confidence in assessment findings and is the main objective of the assessment review. Part of the assessment review also includes understanding the impact of the identified deficiencies on the organization's operations, assets, and individuals.
>
> **Subtask 6.2:** Determine if the risk to the organization's operations, assets, or potentially affected individuals is acceptable, and arrive at an accreditation decision.
>
> **Responsibility:** DAA
>
> **Guidance:** After the completion of the assessment review, the DAA has a clear understanding of the impact of deficiencies. This helps the DAA to judge which deficiencies are of greatest concern to the organization and which can be tolerated without creating unreasonable organization-level risk. The CAP is also considered in determining the risk to the organization in terms of when and how the OIMO intends to address the known deficiencies. The DAA may consult the OIMO, Assessor, or other organization officials before completing the final risk evaluation. This risk evaluation in turn determines the degree of acceptability of PCI operations. The logic for using the latter as the basis for an accreditation decision is described in Section 2.9.

Task 7: Accreditation Documentation

The accreditation documentation task includes— (i) completing and transmitting the accreditation decision package to the appropriate individuals and organizations; and (ii) updating the PCI's operations plan.

Subtask 7.1: Provide copies of the accreditation decision package, in either paper or electronic form, to the OIMO and any other organization officials having interests, roles, or responsibilities in the PCI.

Responsibility: DAA

Guidance: The accreditation decision package, including the accreditation decision letter, should be transmitted to the OIMO. Upon receipt of the accreditation decision package, the OIMO must review the authorization and its terms and conditions. The original accreditation decision package must be kept on file by the OIMO. The DAA shall retain copies of the contents of the accreditation decision package. The accreditation decision package must be appropriately safeguarded and stored, whenever possible, in a centralized organization filing system to ensure accessibility. The accreditation decision package shall be available to authorized auditors and oversight organizations upon request. The accreditation decision package must be retained in accordance with the organization's records retention policy. The PCI and specific facilities are accredited for a maximum of three (3) years from the date of the ATO. After the period ends, re-accreditation must be performed.

Subtask 7.2: Update the PCI's operations plan.

Responsibility: OIMO

Guidance: The operations plan must be updated to reflect all changes made as the result of assessment and accreditation. All conditions of PCI operations that are set forth in the accreditation decision must also be noted in the plan.

5.4 Monitoring Phase

The Monitoring Phase consists of two tasks— (i) operations plan maintenance; and (ii) annual lifecycle walkthrough. Based on the importance of reliably creating and issuing PIV Cards, it is imperative that once the accreditation is completed, the PCI is monitored to ensure that policies, procedures, and processes remain in effect as originally intended. There can be significant changes in a PCI's policies, management, operations personnel, and available technology during a three-year ATO. These changes must be monitored so that the organization minimizes exposing itself to security and privacy threats existing or arising in the PCI. For example, if there is a significant staff turnover in the PCI, the organization must be sure that the new PCI staff is enrolling applicants and issuing cards using the same reliable processes that were previously approved.

In order to facilitate the monitoring of a PCI without undue burden in activities and paperwork, only two activities are required during this phase: maintenance of the operations plan and an annual lifecycle walkthrough of PCI operations. The latter entails reviewing all the services and functions of a PCI and its facilities for continued reliability. The annual walkthrough must cover a PIV Card's lifecycle from sponsorship to maintenance. Observation of the full lifecycle of a card ensures that all processes are still reliably operating as assessed during the accreditation.

Task 8: Operations Plan Update

A PCI's operations plan is the primary description of what and how PIV Card issuing services are provided. It is essential that this document be updated as changes occur in the PCI's operations. The PCI management will be able to analyze the impact of changes as they occur and will be significantly better prepared when re-accreditation is required.

>**Subtask 8.1:** Document all relevant changes in the PCI within the operations plan.
>
>**Responsibility:** OIMO
>
>**Guidance:** In addition to the policies, procedures, and processes that must be documented if changes are made, the organization shall update the operations plan if changes to the PCI information system, the PIV Card, privacy policies, roles and responsibilities, or PCI controls are made.
>
>**Subtask 8.2:** Analyze the proposed or actual changes to the PCI and determine the impact of such changes.
>
>**Responsibility:** OIMO
>
>**Guidance:** If the results of the impact analysis indicate that changes to the PCI could affect the reliability of the PCI's operations, the changes and impact on the PCI must be reported to the DAA, corrective actions must be initiated, and the CAP must be updated. In instances where major changes have occurred, the PCI must be re-accredited.

Task 9: Annual Lifecycle Walkthrough

The annual lifecycle walkthrough is a monitoring activity to be performed initially by the PCI when its PIV Card issuing services begin, and annually thereafter. The OIMO (or designated appointee) is responsible for observing and reviewing the entire lifecycle of a PIV Card. This walkthrough should provide an accurate snapshot of the PCI's operations and reliability at a point in time. By walking through the PIV Card lifecycle, from sponsorship to issuance, including maintenance, the operations of the PCI can be examined as an integrated entity. During the walkthrough, the OIMO (or designated appointee) shall observe all processes involving the PIV Card, comparing them against the requirements defined in the PCI controls. This activity shall be performed every year after each accreditation until re-accreditation begins. All identified deficiencies in reliable operations shall be sent to the DAA for review and analysis. Any potential impact to the reliability of the PCI's operations and risk to the organization shall be documented and presented to the OIMO and the DAA.

>**Subtask 9.1:** Observe all the processes involved in getting a PIV Card, including those from sponsorship to maintenance. Observe each process and compare its controls against the applicable list of required PCI controls. If a PCI has several facilities, this process should be repeated using randomly selected PCIFs.

Responsibility: OIMO (or designated appointee)

Guidance: As part of the walkthrough, the OIMO (or designated appointee) observes the processes followed for new employees and contractors (if different) as well as PIV Card maintenance processes, such as card termination, reissuance, or renewals. The OIMO (or designated appointee) observes each process and compares it against the documented steps for the PCI and the associated PCI controls. An annual walkthrough is required until re-accreditation is initiated.

Subtask 9.2: The results of the lifecycle walkthrough are summarized in a report to the DAA. Deficiencies must be highlighted, along with corrective actions that must be implemented to correct any deficiencies.

Responsibility: OIMO, DAA

Guidance: The OIMO (or designated appointee) shall document the results of the walkthrough. The results shall be recorded in the assessment report template included in Appendix E. All deficiencies should be highlighted, and a plan for correcting each deficiency shall be documented. The DAA shall decide if any deficiency is significant enough to require a change of the PCI's authorization-to-operate status.

APPENDIX A: REFERENCES

S. 3418 [5 U.S.C. § 552A through Public Law 93-579], 93rd U.S. Cong., 2d Sess., *The Privacy Act of 1974*, December 31, 1974 (effective September 27, 1975).
(Available at http://www.archives.gov/research_room/foia_reading_room/privacy_act/privacy_act.html.)

H.R. 2458, Title III [Public Law 107-347], 107th U.S. Cong., 2d Sess., *Federal Information Security Management Act of 2002*, December 17, 2002.
(Available at http://frwebgate.access.gpo.gov/cgi-bin/getdoc.cgi?dbname=107_cong_public_laws&docid=f:publ347.107.pdf.)

Committee for National Security Systems, Instruction 4009, *National Information Assurance Glossary*, Revised May 2003.
(Available at http://staff.washington.edu/dittrich/center/4009.pdf.)

Executive Office of the President, Executive Order 10450, *Security Requirements for Government Employees*, April 17, 1953.
(Available at http://www.archives.gov/federal-register/codification/executive-order/10450.html.)

Executive Office of the President, Homeland Security Presidential Directive 12, Policy for a Common Identification Standard for Federal Employees and Contractors, August 27, 2004.
(Available at http://www.whitehouse.gov/news/releases/2004/08/20040827-8.html.)

Federal Identity Credentialing Committee, *Federal Identity Management Handbook*, Version 0.1, December 2005.
(Available at http://www.cio.gov/ficc/documents/FederalIdentityManagementHandbook.pdf.)

United States Department of Commerce, National Institute of Standards and Technology, Draft Federal Information Processing Standards Publication 140-3, *Security Requirements for Cryptographic Modules*, July 2007.
(Available at http://csrc.nist.gov/publications/PubsDrafts.html#FIPS-140-3.)

United States Department of Commerce, National Institute of Standards and Technology, Federal Information Processing Standards Publication 199, *Standards for Security Categorization of Federal Information and Information Systems*, February 2004.
(Available at http://csrc.nist.gov/publications/fips/fips199/FIPS-PUB-199-final.pdf.)

United States Department of Commerce, National Institute of Standards and Technology, Federal Information Processing Standards Publication 200, *Security Controls for Federal Information Systems*, March 2006.
(Available at http://csrc.nist.gov/publications/fips/fips200/FIPS-200-final-march.pdf.)

United States Department of Commerce, National Institute of Standards and Technology, Federal Information Processing Standards Publication 201-1, *Personal Identity Verification of Federal Employees and Contractors*, March 2006.
(Available at http://csrc.nist.gov/publications/fips/fips201-1/FIPS-201-1-chng1.pdf.)

United States Department of Commerce, National Institute of Standards and Technology, Special Publication 800-37, *Guide for the Security Certification and Accreditation of Federal Information Systems*, Version 2.0, May 2004.
(Available at http://csrc.nist.gov/publications/nistpubs/800-37/SP800-37-final.pdf.)

United States Department of Commerce, National Institute of Standards and Technology, Special Publication 800-53 Rev. 1, *Recommended Security Controls for Federal Information Systems*, December 2006.
(Available at http://csrc.nist.gov/publications/nistpubs/800-53-Rev1/800-53-rev1-final-clean-sz.pdf.)

United States Department of Commerce, National Institute of Standards and Technology, Special Publication 800-59, *Guideline for Identifying an Information System as a National Security System*, August 2003.
(Available at http://csrc.nist.gov/publications/nistpubs/800-59/SP800-59.pdf.)

United States Department of Commerce, National Institute of Standards and Technology, Draft Special Publication 800-73-2, *Interfaces for Personal Identity Verification*, October 2007.
(Available at http://csrc.nist.gov/publications/PubsDrafts.html#SP-800-73--2.)

United States Department of Commerce, National Institute of Standards and Technology, Special Publication 800-76-1, *Biometric Data Specification for Personal Identity Verification*, January 2007.
(Available at http://csrc.nist.gov/publications/nistpubs/800-76-1/SP800-76-1_012407.pdf.)

United States Department of Commerce, National Institute of Standards and Technology, Special Publication 800-78-1, *Cryptographic Algorithms and Key Sizes for Personal Identity Verification*, August 2007.
(Available at http://csrc.nist.gov/publications/nistpubs/800-78-1/SP-800-78-1_final2.pdf.)

United States Department of Commerce, National Institute of Standards and Technology, Special Publication 800-85A, *PIV Card Application and Middleware Interface Test Guidelines (SP 800-73 Compliance)*, April 2006.
(Available at http://csrc.nist.gov/publications/nistpubs/800-85A/SP800-85A.pdf.)

United States Department of Commerce, National Institute of Standards and Technology, Special Publication 800-85B, *PIV Data Model Test Guidelines*, July 2006.
(Available at http://csrc.nist.gov/publications/nistpubs/800-85B/SP800-85b-072406-final.pdf.)

United States Department of Commerce, National Institute of Standards and Technology, Special Publication 800-104, *A Scheme for PIV Visual Card Topography*, June 2007.
(Available at http://csrc.nist.gov/publications/nistpubs/800-104/SP800-104-June29_2007-final.pdf.)

United States Department of Commerce, National Institute of Standards and Technology, Draft Interagency Report 7328, *Security Assessment Provider Requirements and Customer Responsibilities: Building a Security Assessment Credentialing Program for Federal Information Systems*, September 2007.
(Available at http://csrc.nist.gov/publications/PubsDrafts.html#NIST-IR-7328.)

United States Office of Management and Budget, *Circular No. A-130 Revised*, Appendix III, Security of Federal Automated Information Resources, February 1996.
(Available at http://www.whitehouse.gov/omb/circulars/a130/a130appendix_iii.html.)

APPENDIX B: GLOSSARY AND ACRONYMS

Terms/Acronyms used in this document	Definition or explanation of terms; expansion of acronyms
Access Control	The process of granting or denying specific requests to: (i) obtain and use information and related information processing services; and (ii) enter specific physical facilities (e.g., Federal buildings, military establishments, and border-crossing entrances).
Accreditation (as applied to a PCI)	The official management decision of the Designated Accreditation Authority to authorize operation of a PCI after determining that the PCI's reliability has satisfactorily being established through appropriate assessment processes.
Accreditation Package	The results of assessment and supporting documentation provided to the Designated Accreditation Authority to be used in the accreditation decision process.
Agency	An executive department specified in 5 U.S.C., Sec. 101; a military department specified in 5 U.S.C., Sec. 102; an independent establishment as defined in 5 U.S.C., Sec. 104(1); or a wholly owned Government corporation fully subject to the provisions of 31 U.S.C., Chapter 91.
Applicant	An individual applying for a PIV Card.
Assessment (as applied to a PCI)	Assessment in this context means a formal process of assessing the implementation and reliable use of PCI controls using various methods of assessment (e.g., interviews, document reviews, observations) that support the assertion that a PCI is reliably meeting the requirements of FIPS 201-1.
Assessment Method	A focused activity or action employed by an Assessor for evaluating a particular PCI control.
Assessment Procedure	A set of activities or actions employed by an Assessor to determine the extent that a PCI control is implemented and used by a PCI.
Assessor	The individual responsible for conducting assessment activities under the guidance and direction of a Designated Accreditation Authority.
ATO	Authorization to Operate; One of three possible decisions concerning a PCI made by a Designated Accreditation Authority after all assessment activities have been performed stating that the reliability of the PCI is accredited and the PCI is authorized to perform specific PIV Card services.
CAP (Corrective Action Plan)	Corrective actions of a PCI for removing or reducing deficiencies or risks during PCI operations. The plan identifies actions that need to be performed in order to obtain or sustain accreditation.
Card Activation/Issuance	A process that includes the procurement of FIPS-approved blank identity cards, initializing them using appropriate software and data elements for identity verification and access control applications, personalization of the cards with the identity credentials of authorized subjects, and delivery of the personalized cards to the

Terms/Acronyms used in this document	Definition or explanation of terms; expansion of acronyms
	authorized subjects, along with appropriate instructions for protection and use.
Component	An element, such as a fingerprint capture station or card reader within the PCI, for which FIPS 201-1 makes specific requirements.
Credential	Evidence attesting to one's right to credit or authority; in FIPS 201-1, it is the PIV Card and data elements associated with an individual that authoritatively binds an identity (and, optionally, additional attributes) to that individual.
DAA	Designated Accreditation Authority; A senior organization official that has been given the authorization to accredit the reliability of a PCI.
DATO	Denial of Authorization to Operate; issued by a DAA to a PCI that is not accredited as being reliable for the issuance of PIV Cards.
Enrollment/Identity Proofing	The process that includes: (i) identity proofing and (ii) making a person's identity known to the PCI information system by associating a unique identifier with that identity, and collecting and recording the person's relevant attributes into the PCI information system. Enrollment is necessary in order to initiate other processes, such as adjudication, card issuance and maintenance, that are necessary to issue and maintain a PIV Card.
FIPS	Federal Information Processing Standard
HSPD	Homeland Security Presidential Directive; HSPD-12 established the policy for which FIPS 201-1 was developed.
IATO	Interim Authorization to Operate a PCI performing specified services (e.g., enrollment/identity proofing, card production, card activation/issuance and maintenance).
Identification	The process of discovering the true identity (i.e., origin, initial history) of a person or item from the entire collection of similar persons or items.
Identifier	Unique data used to represent a person's identity and associated attributes. A name or a card number are examples of identifiers.
Identity	The set of physical and behavioral characteristics by which an individual is uniquely recognizable.
Identity Proofing	Verifying the claimed identity of an applicant by authenticating the identity source documents provided by the applicant.
ITL	Information Technology Laboratory
Maintenance	The process of managing PIV Cards once they are issued. It includes termination, renewal and re-issuance.
NIST	National Institute of Standards and Technology
OIMO	Organization Identity Management Official; The individual responsible for overseeing the operations of a PCI in accordance with FIPS 201-1 and for performing the responsibilities specified in this guideline.

Terms/Acronyms used in this document	Definition or explanation of terms; expansion of acronyms
OMB	Office of Management and Budget
PCI	PIV Card Issuer
PCI information system	A computer-based system used by a PCI to perform the functions necessary for PIV Card issuance as per FIPS 201-1.
PCIF	PCI Facility
PII	Personally Identifiable Information; Any representation of information that permits the identity of an individual to whom the information applies to be reasonably inferred by either direct or indirect means. [E-Gov]
PIV	Personal Identity Verification as specified in FIPS 201-1.
PIV Card	The physical artifact (e.g., identity card, "smart" card) issued to an applicant by a PCI that contains stored identity markers or credentials (e.g., a photograph, cryptographic keys, digitized fingerprint representations) so that the claimed identity of the cardholder can be verified against the stored credentials by another person (human readable and verifiable) or an automated process (computer readable and verifiable).
PO	Privacy Official
Risk	The level of potential impact on an organization operations (including mission, functions, image, or reputation), organization assets, or individuals of a threat or a given likelihood of that threat occurring.
SAO	Senior Authorizing Official; A senior organization official that has budgetary control, provides oversight, develops policy, and has authority over all functions and services provided by the PCI
SOP	Standard operating procedures
SOR	A system of records is a group of records under the control of a Federal agency which contains a personal identifier (such as a name, date of birth, finger print, Social Security Number, and Employee Number) and one other item of personal data (such as home address, performance rating, and blood type) from which information is retrieved using a personal identifier.
SORN	The Privacy Act requires each agency to publish a notice if its systems of records in the Federal Register. This is called a System of Record Notice (SORN).
SP	Special Publication

APPENDIX C: PCI READINESS REVIEW CHECKLIST

The readiness review checklist may be used by a PCI preparing for assessment and accreditation by an assessment team. The checklist may also be used to validate that the PCI has collected all relevant documentation, identified appropriate individuals with knowledge of the PCI and made them available, and provided access to the PCI to the assessment team.

Activity	Completed?	Comments
• Identify an independent assessment team to assess the PCI.		
• Determine the accreditation boundary.		
• Establish the scope and objectives of the assessment.		
• Determine the level of effort and resources necessary to carry out the assessment.		
• Establish the time-frame to complete the assessment and identify key milestone decision points.		
• Notify key personnel at the PCI Facility and any external service providers (if applicable) of the impending assessment.		
• Validate that the PCI operations plan is complete and includes all the required information.		
• Ensure that the necessary roles within the PCI have been designated.		
• Validate that implementation and management responsibility for PCI controls have been accurately assigned.		
• Make sure that the information systems utilized by the PCI have been certified and accredited to operate in accordance with SP 800-37.		
• Ensure that the following documentation has been developed and can be made available to the assessment team: (i) PCI operations plan (ii) Results from any past assessment and accreditation decisions for the PCI (iii) Letters of appointment (if any) (iv) Service Level Agreements (SLA) and Memorandums of Understanding (MOU) between the organization and the service provider(s).		

Activity	Completed?	Comments
(v) Listing of all HSPD-12 components used within the PIV system (vi) Privacy-related documentation (vii) All forms utilized within the PCI (viii) Documentation from outsourced providers (ix) Standard operating procedures for the PCI Facilities within the accreditation boundary for the PCI (x) Signed accreditation letter under SP 800-37 for each information system within the PCI		
• The PIV system is operational and actual PIV processes can be observed by the assessment team.		
• The PIV system is in production and operational. PIV Cards are being or ready to be produced that can be used for testing by the assessment team.		

APPENDIX D: PCI OPERATIONS PLAN TEMPLATE

The following is a suggested outline for the PCI operations plan. It is highly recommended that an organization follow this template to document its PCI operations comprehensively and to the full extent as needed to support a successful accreditation.

I. Background

<Provide a brief background on HSPD-12, FIPS 201-1 and PIV, as well as how the organization has planned to meet the Directive.>

II. Purpose and Scope

<Describe the purpose and scope of the operations plan.>

III. Applicable Laws, Directives, Policies, Regulations & Standards

<Identify all Laws, Directives, Policies, Regulations and Standards that govern PIV Card issuance at the Organization.>

IV. PCI Roles and Responsibilities

<Identify the accreditation-related roles and responsibilities of all key personnel within the PCI.>

V. Assignment of Roles

<Document how the various roles that have been identified in the section above are appointed. These can be either specific individuals or positions within the organization. Provide contact information for all the roles assigned.>

VI. PCI Description

<Provide a description of the organization's PCI. Details such as structure and geographic dispersion should be included.>

VII. PCI Facility Details

<Identify all the PCI Facilities that are included within the PCI that are part of the accreditation boundary. Provide details such as the location, PIV Card functions performed (e.g. enrollment and/or registration) at the facility and the approximate number of PIV Cards supported at each facility.>

VIII. PCI Management

<This section discusses various management aspects of the PCI.>

a. Coordination and Interaction
<Describe management interactions within the PCI, both at an organization level, and between the organization and the facility(s).>

b. Staffing
<Describe the procedures employed to make sure that adequate staff is available for performing PIV Card related functions.>

c. Training
<Describe the procedures employed to ensure that the staff is properly trained to perform their respective duties.>

d. Procurement
<Describe the mechanism typically used for procuring products/services related to the organization's HSPD-12 implementation.>

e. Outsourcing
<Describe the PIV Card functions being outsourced at the PCI (if applicable).>

IX. PCI Policies and Procedures

<Describe in this section the various policies and procedures that apply for (i) sponsorship, (ii) Enrollment and Identity proofing, (iii)Adjudication, (iv) card production, (v) card activation and issuance and (vi) maintenance. Also discuss the procedures for temporary badges, as well as for non-PIV badges employed by the organization. >

a. Sponsorship
b. Enrollment/Identity Proofing
c. Adjudication
d. Card Production
e. Card Activation/Issuance
f. Maintenance
   i. Card Termination
   ii. Card Renewal
   iii. Card Re-issuance
b. Temporary/Non-PIV Badges

X. PCI Information System (s) Description

<Provide a description of the technical aspects of the organization's PIV system, including system architecture, network connectivity, connections to external system and information shared both internally and externally, the PKI provider as well as the information system accreditation status. >

a. Architecture
b. Interconnections and Information Sharing
c. Information System Inventory
d. Public Key Infrastructure
e. SP 800-37 C&A Information

XI. Card Personalization & Production

<Describe the organization's PIV Card graphical layout(s), as well the optional data containers being used. Provide details if there are any PIV Card expiration date requirements levied by the organization. Also describe the mechanisms in place for securing both pre-personalized and personalized PIV Card stock >

a. PIV Card Graphical Topology
b. PIV Card Electronic Data Elements
c. Expiration Date Requirements
d. Card Inventory Management

XII. Card Reporting Requirements

<Describe how the organization collects information from its facilities relating to the number of PIV Cards issued, background investigations completed etc, as required by OMB. Also provide detail on how the organization consolidates this information and provides its report to OMB on the status of their HSPD-12 implementation. >

XIII. PCI Controls

<This section documents the PCI Controls and provides the following information for each: (i) PCI control identifier and description, (ii) control owner, (iii) whether the control is organization-specific or facility-specific and (iv) a description of how the PCI control has been implemented by the organization. >

a. PCI Control Identifier and Description
b. PCI Control Owner
c. Organization/Facility Specific
d. How the PCI control is implemented

Appendix A - Memoranda of Appointment

<Attached copies of signed memoranda-of-appointment that record the various roles that have been assigned and the personnel fulfilling these roles that have accepted the position and its associated responsibilities. >

Appendix B - Privacy Requirements

<Attached copies of the privacy-related information as identified below. >

a. Privacy Policy
b. Privacy Impact Assessment
c. System of Record Notice
d. Privacy Act Statement/Notice
e. Rules of Conduct
f. Privacy Processes
    i. Requests to review personal information
    ii. Requests to amend personal information
    iii. Appeal procedures
    iv. Complaint procedures

Appendix C – Service Level Agreements, Memoranda of Understanding (MOU)

<Attached copies of any service level agreements and memoranda of understanding executed between the organization and any external service provider that has been contracted to provide certain PIV related functions.>

APPENDIX E: ASSESSMENT REPORT TEMPLATE

Below is a template to use when generating the assessment report. This is to be completed for each PCI control. An example using a specific PCI control follows.

Accreditation Focus Area

PCI Control Identifier—

PCI Control Description—

PCI Control Owner / Control Level — (External Service Provider, Organization specific, Facility specific)

Assessment Result— (Satisfied, Partially Satisfied, Not Satisfied, Not Applicable)

Assessment Findings—

Assessment Deficiency and Potential Impact—

Recommendation—

Card Activation/Issuance Process

PCI Control Identifier— AI-7

PCI Control Description— The issuer performs a 1:1 biometric match of the applicant against the biometric included in the PIV Card or in the enrollment record. On a successful match, the PIV Card may be released to the applicant

PCI Control Owner— External Service Provider, Facility Specific

Assessment Result— Partially Satisfied

Assessment Findings— There is operational evidence that a 1:1 biometric match is carried out before the card is released to the applicant.

Assessment Deficiency and Potential Impact— The requirement to carry out this task is not documented clearly enough in the operations plan. Although personnel are knowledgeable about this requirement, and the task was observed to be performed correctly during card issuance, the lack of documentation could be a problem if there is turnover in staff.

Recommendation— Update the issuance process description within the operations plan to include a clear description of this task in the process.

Summary Report Template

PAT (% Satisfied, % Partially Satisfied, % Not Satisfied)

For each Accreditation Focus Area

(% PCI controls Satisfied, % Partially Satisfied, % Not Satisfied)

(% Review Assessments Satisfied, % Interview Assessments Satisfied, % Observe Assessments Satisfied, % Test Assessments Satisfied)

APPENDIX F: SAMPLE TRANSMITTAL AND DECISION LETTERS

Sample Assessment/Accreditation Package Transmittal Letter

From: Organization Identity Management Official   Date:

To: Designated Accreditation Authority (DAA)

Subject: PCI Accreditation Package for [PCI]

An assessment of the [PCI NAME] located at [PCI Location and PCIF Locations] has been conducted in accordance with NIST Special Publication (SP) 800-79-1, *Guidelines for the Accreditation of PIV Card Issuers* and the [ORGANIZATION] policy on PCI accreditation. The attached accreditation package contains— (i) the PCI operations plan; (ii) the assessment report; (iii) a corrective actions plan (CAP); and (iv) An SP 800-37 accreditation letter for each information system within the PCI.

The PCI operations plan, its policies, procedures, and processes have been assessed by [ASSESSOR] using the assessment methods and procedures defined in SP 800-79-1 and specified in the assessment report to determine the extent to which the requirements under HSPD-12 and FIPS 201-1 are exhibited. The CAP describes the corrective actions that we plan to perform to remove or reduce any remaining deficiencies detected in the PCI's operations.

Signature

Title

Sample Accreditation Decision Letter (Authorization to Operate)

From: Designated Accreditation Authority   Date:

To: Organization Identity Management Official

Subject: Accreditation Decision for [PCI]

After reviewing the results of the accreditation package of the [PCI], I have determined that the PCI's policies, procedures, and processes are in compliance both with FIPS 201-1 and our organization's own policies, regulations and standards. Accordingly, I am issuing an *authorization to operate* (ATO) the PCI's services. The PCI is accredited without any restrictions or limitations. This accreditation is my formal declaration that the requirements of HSPD-12 are being satisfied by the PCI.

This ATO also applies to facilities under the PCI. Included is a list of facilities authorized to operate under this accreditation decision.

This accreditation and ATO will remain in effect for 3 years from the date of this letter if— (i) all required documentation is updated annually; (ii) a lifecycle walkthrough is completed annually and the results sent to me within thirty (30) days of completion; and (iii) no deficiencies are identified during the walkthrough that would increase the risk to the organization's mission.

A copy of this letter and all supporting accreditation documentation shall be retained in accordance with the organization's record retention schedule.

Signature

Title

Sample Accreditation Decision Letter (Interim Authorization to Operate)

From: Designated Accreditation Authority   Date:

To: Organization Identity Management Official

Subject: Accreditation Decision for [PCI]

After reviewing the results of the assessment of the [PCI], I have determined that the PCI does not satisfy the requirements identified in FIPS 201-1 and the organization's policies, regulations, and standards. However, I have determined that there is an overarching need for the PCI to provide the needed services due to mission necessity and other considerations. Accordingly, I am issuing an *interim authorization to operate* (IATO) the PCI's services. Operation of the PCI must be performed in accordance with the enclosed terms and conditions during the IATO period. The PCI is *not* considered accredited during the IATO period.

This IATO also applies to facilities under the PCI. Included is a list of facilities authorized to operate during this interim period, along with specific limitations or restrictions that apply.

This interim authorization to operate is valid for a maximum till close of business on <date> [not to exceed three months]. This interim authorization will remain in effect as long as— (i) the required status reports for the PCI are submitted to this office every month; (ii) the problems or deficiencies reported from the accreditation do not result in additional risk that is deemed unacceptable; and (iii) continued progress is being made in reducing or eliminating the deficiencies in accordance with the corrective actions plan (CAP). At the end of IATO period, the PCI must either be accredited and authorized to operate, or the authorization for further operation will be denied. A second IATO will be granted only in extenuating circumstances. This office will review the CAP submitted with the accreditation package during the IATO period and monitor progress on removal or reduction of concerns and discrepancies before re-accreditation is initiated.

A copy of this letter and all supporting accreditation documentation shall be retained in accordance with the organization's record retention schedule.

Signature

Title

Sample Accreditation Decision Letter (Denial of Authorization to Operate)

From: Designated Accreditation Authority   Date:

To: Organization Identity Management Official

Subject: Accreditation Decision for [PCI]

After reviewing the results of the assessment of the [PCI] and the supporting evidence provided in the associated accreditation package, I have determined that the requirements identified in FIPS 201-1 and the organization's policies, regulations, and standards are not being exhibited by the PCI. Accordingly, I am issuing a denial of authorization to operate (DATO) to the PCI and its facilities. The PCI is *not* accredited and [MAY NOT BE PLACED INTO OPERATION or ALL CURRENT OPERATIONS MUST BE HALTED].

The corrective actions plan (CAP) is to be pursued immediately to ensure that proactive measures are taken to correct the deficiencies found during the assessment. Re- accreditation is to be initiated at the earliest opportunity to determine the effectiveness of correcting the deficiencies.

A copy of this letter and all supporting accreditation documentation shall be retained in accordance with the organization's record retention schedule.

Signature

Title

APPENDIX G: PCI CONTROLS AND ASSESSMENT PROCEDURES

PAT = Organizational Preparedness			
Accreditation Focus Area	**Identifier**	**PCI Control**	**Source**

Preparation and Maintenance of Documentation	DO-1	The organization develops and implements a PCI operations plan according to the template in Appendix D. The operations plan references other documents as needed.
		
		Assessment
		Determine that:
		  (i) *the operations plan includes the relevant elements from the template in Appendix D (review);*
		  (ii) *the operations plan includes the list of PCI controls and the PCI control owner for each, how they were implemented and whether they are organization or facility specific (review);*
		  (iii) *documentation that is not included in the operations plan is referenced accurately (review);*
		  (iv) *the operations plan has been reviewed and approved by the DAA within the organization (review, interview).*
			SP 800-79-1, Section 2.11 – Accreditation Package and Supporting Documentation

	DO-2	The organization has a written policy and procedures for enrollment/identity proofing that are approved by the head of the organization.
		
		Assessment
		Determine that:
		  (i) *the organization has developed and documented written policy and procedures for identity proofing and enrollment for personnel requiring a PIV Card (e.g. employees, contractors and foreign nationals) (review);*
		  (ii) *the policy is consistent with the organization's mission and functions, FIPS 201-1 and applicable laws, directives, policies, regulations, standards, and guidance (review);*
		  (iii) *the policy and procedures have been signed off by the head of the organization (review);*
		  (iv) *the organization will periodically review and update the policy and procedures as required (review, interview).*
			FIPS 201-1, Section 2.2 – PIV Identity Proofing and Registration Requirements

	DO-3	The organization has a written policy and procedures for issuance that are approved by the head of the organization.
		
		Assessment
		Determine that:
		  (i) *the organization has developed and documented a written policy and procedures for issuance (review);*
		  (ii) *the policy is consistent with the organization's mission and functions, FIPS 201-1 and applicable laws, directives, policies, regulations, standards, and guidance (review);*
		  (iii) *the policy and procedures have been signed off by the head of the organization (review);*
		  (iv) *the organization will periodically review and update the policy and procedures as required (review, interview).*
			FIPS 201-1, Section 2.3 – PIV Issuance and Maintenance Requirements

		PAT = Organizational Preparedness	
Accreditation Focus Area	Identifier	PCI Control	Source
	DO-4	The organization has a written policy and procedures descr bing the conditions for PIV Card renewal that are approved by the head of the organization. **Assessment** *Determine that:* (i) *the organization has developed and documented a written policy and procedures for card renewal (review);* (ii) *the policy is consistent with the organization's mission and functions, FIPS 201-1 and applicable laws, directives, policies, regulations, standards, and guidance (review);* (iii) *the policy and procedures have been signed off by the head of the organization (review);* (iv) *the organization will periodically review and update the policy and procedures as required (review, interview).*	FIPS 201-1, Section 5.3.2.1 – PIV Card Renewal
	DO-5	The organization has a written policy and procedures descr bing the conditions for PIV Card termination that are approved by the head of the organization. **Assessment** *Determine that:* (i) *the organization has developed and documented a written policy and procedures for PIV Card termination (review);* (ii) *the policy is consistent with the organization's mission and functions, FIPS 201-1 and applicable laws, directives, policies, regulations, standards, and guidance (review);* (iii) *the policy and procedures have been signed off by the head of the organization (review);* (iv) *the organization will periodically review and update the policy as required (review, interview).*	FIPS 201-1 Section 5.3.2.4 - – PIV Card Termination
	DO-6	The organization has a written policy and procedures descr bing the conditions for PIV Card re-issuance that are approved by the head of the organization. **Assessment** *Determine that:* (i) *the organization has developed and documented a written policy and procedures for re-issuance (review);* (ii) *the policy is consistent with the organization's mission and functions, FIPS 201-1 and applicable laws, directives, policies, regulations, standards, and guidance (review);* (iii) *the policy and procedures have been signed off by the head of the organization (review);* (iv) *the organization will periodically review and update the policy and procedures as required (review, interview).*	FIPS 201-1 Section 5.3.2.2 – PIV Card Reissuance
	DO-7	In cases where a PIV Card is not required, such as temporary employees and contractors employed for less than 6 months and visitors, the organization has a written policy and procedures describing the conditions for temporary badges. **Assessment** *Determine that:* (i) *the organization has developed and documented a written policy and procedures for the issuance of temporary badges (review);* (ii) *the policy is consistent with the organization's mission and functions, FIPS 201-1 and applicable laws, directives, policies, regulations, standards, and guidance (review);* (iii) *the organization will periodically review and update the policy and procedures as required (review, interview).*	OMB Memorandum 05-24

| \multicolumn{4}{c}{PAT = Organizational Preparedness} |
Accreditation Focus Area	Identifier	PCI Control	Source
Assignment of Roles and Responsbilities	RR-1	The organization has appointed the role of Senior Authorizing Official (SAO). **Assessment** *Determine that:* *(i) the organization has defined the role of Senior Authorizing Official and its responsibilities according to the requirements of SP 800-79-1 (review);* *(ii) the organization has assigned the role of Senior Authorizing Official (review);*	SP 800-79-1, Section 2.6 – Roles and Responsbilities
	RR-2	The organization has appointed the role of Designated Accreditation Authority (DAA). **Assessment** *Determine that:* *(i) the organization has defined the role of Designated Accreditation Authority and its responsibilities according to the requirements of SP 800-79-1 (review);* *(ii) the organization has assigned the role of Designated Accreditation Authority (review, interview);*	SP 800-79-1, Section 2.6 – Roles and Responsbilities
	RR-3	The organization has appointed the role of Organization Identity Management Official (OIMO). **Assessment** *Determine that:* *(i) the organization has defined the role of Organization Identity Management Official and its responsibilities according to the requirements of SP 800-79-1 (interview);* *(ii) the organization has assigned the role of Organization Identity Management Official (review, interview).*	SP 800-79-1, Section 2.6 – Roles and Responsbilities
	RR-4	The organization has appointed the role of Assessor. **Assessment** *Determine that:* *(i) the organization has defined the role of Assessor and its responsibilities according to the requirements of SP 800-79-1 (review);* *(ii) the organization has assigned the role of Assessor (review);* *(iii) the Assessor is independent of, and organizationally separate from, the persons and office(s) directly responsible for the day-to-day operation of the organization (review, interview).*	SP 800-79-1, Section 2.6 – Roles and Responsbilities
	RR-5	The organization has appointed the role of Privacy Official (PO). **Assessment** *Determine that:* *(i) the organization has defined the role of Privacy Official and its responsibilities according to the requirements of SP 800-79-1 (review);* *(ii) the organization has assigned the role of Privacy Official in the operations plan (review, interview);* *(iii) the Privacy Official does not have any other roles in the PCI (review, interview).*	SP 800-79-1, Section 2.6 – Roles and Responsbilities

| \multicolumn{4}{c}{PAT = Organizational Preparedness} |
Accreditation Focus Area	Identifier	PCI Control	Source
	RR-6	The PCI Facility employs processes which adhere to the principle of separation of duties to ensure that no single individual has the capability to issue a PIV Card without the cooperation of another authorized person. **Assessment** *Determine that:* (i) *the PCI facility standard operating procedures document the principle of separation of duties (review);* (ii) *the PCI facility's processes demonstrate adherence to the principle of separation of duties (interview, observe).*	FIPS 201-1, Section 5.2 – PIV Identity Proofing and Registration
Facility and Personnel Readiness	**Facility**		
	FP-1	Minimum physical controls at the PCI Facility are implemented. These include: (i) use of locked rooms, safes, and cabinets (as appropriate); (ii) physical access to key areas within the facility is restricted to authorized personnel, (iii) security monitoring and automated alarms are implemented, (iv) emergency power and lighting are available, and (v) fire prevention and protection mechanisms are implemented. **Assessment** *Determine that:* (i) *the OIMO and PCIF Managers(s) are aware of the minimum set of physical controls that need to be in place at the facility(ies) (interview);* (ii) *the minimum physical security controls are implemented by the PCI Facility (observe).*	Commonly accepted security readiness measures
	FP-2	PCI Documentation (e.g., operations plan, standard operating procedures, and contracts) are maintained at each PCI Facility. **Assessment** *Determine that:* (i) *the most current versions of the PCI documentation is available at the PCI Facility for reference as needed (interview, review);*	Commonly accepted security readiness measures
	Equipment		
	FP-3	The PCIF Manager(s) has a copy of the contingency/disaster recovery plan for the information systems, which is stored securely. **Assessment** *Determine that:* (i) *the contingency plan/ disaster recovery plan is stored* (ii) *securely at the facility (interview, observe);* (iii) *the PCIF Manager is knowledgeable on how to restore/reconstitute the information systems in case of system failures (interview).*	Commonly accepted security readiness measures
	FP-4	The information systems are managed using a system development life cycle (SDLC) methodology that includes information security considerations **Assessment** *Determine that:* (i) *the information system used by the organization has been developed using an SDLC methodology (review, interview);* (ii) *information system security is considered as part of the development life cycle (review).*	Commonly accepted security readiness measures

Accreditation Focus Area	\multicolumn{3}{c}{PAT = Organizational Preparedness}
	Identifier	PCI Control	Source
	FP-5	Enrollment/identity proofing and card activation/issuance workstations are situated in an enclosed area (wall or partition) to provide privacy for an applicant or card holder. **Assessment** *Determine that:* (i) *PCI Facility workstations are situated in an enclosed area (wall or partition) such that other individuals cannot see an applicant or card holder's personal information (observe).*	Commonly accepted security readiness measures
	Key Personnel		
	FP-6	All operators who perform roles within a PCI Facility in the areas of enrollment/ identity proofing or card activation/issuance are allowed access to information systems only when authenticated through a PIV Card. **Assessment** *Determine that:* (i) *the requirement that all operators who perform roles within a PCI Facility in the areas of enrollment/ identity proofing or card activation/issuance are allowed logical access to information systems only when authenticated through a PIV Card, has been documented in the PCI Facility's standard operating procedures (review);* (ii) *Operators use PIV Cards to access information systems in the course of performing their roles in the areas of enrollment/ identity proofing or card activation/issuance access (observe).*	Commonly accepted security readiness measures
	FP-7	All operators who perform roles within a PCI Facility in the areas of enrollment/ identity proofing, adjudication and card activation/issuance have undergone training that is specific to their duties prior to being allowed to perform in that function. **Assessment** *Determine that:* (i) *The requirement that all operators who perform roles within a PCI Facility in the areas of enrollment/ identity proofing, adjudication and card activation/issuance are allowed access to information systems only after completing a training course specific to their duties. (interview, review);* (ii) *Records showing that the appropriate training course has been completed by PCI Facility personnel are stored by the facility for audit purposes (review).*	Commonly accepted security readiness measures
	FP-8	All pre-personalized and personalized smart card stock received from card vendors and card production facilities are received only by authorized personnel who ensure that the card stock is stored securely in the PCI Facility. **Assessment** *Determine that:* (i) *the PCI facility has an authorized list of personnel that are responsible for ensuring that smart card stock is received and stored securely in the PCI Facility (interview);* (ii) *procedures for receiving and storing smart card stock are documented in the PCI Facility's standard operating procedures (review);* (iii) *the authorized personnel are knowledgeable of the procedures on how to receive and store smart card stock (interview).*	Commonly accepted security readiness measures

		PAT = Organizational Preparedness	
Accreditation Focus Area	Identifier	PCI Control	Source
	FP-9	The organization maintains a current list of designated points of contact and alternate points of contact for all PCIFs used by the organization for enrollment/identity proofing and card activation/issuance. **Assessment** *Determine that:* (i) the organization maintains a current list of designated points of contact and alternate points of contact for all PCIFs used by the organization for enrollment/identity proofing and card activation/issuance (review).	Commonly accepted security readiness measures

		PAT = Security Management & Data Protection	
Accreditation Focus Area	Identifier	PCI Control	Source
Protection of Stored and Transmitted Data	ST-1	The PCI information systems that contain information in identifiable form are handled in compliance with Federal laws and policies, including the Privacy Act of 1974. **Assessment** *Determine that:* (i) the PCI Facility does not disclose any record which is contained in the system of records to any person, or to another organization unless written consent has been given by the individual to whom the record pertains unless one of the exceptions for disclosure in the Privacy Act are met (review, interview); (ii) individuals are permitted to gain access to their personal record and the information is provided in a form comprehensible to them (review, interview); (iii) individuals are able to request amendments to records pertaining to them, corrections are made promptly and if not, the individual is provided with a reason for the refusal and is able to request a review of the refusal (review, interview); (iv) the organization notifies an individual when their record is made available to any person under a compulsory legal process when such a process becomes a matter of public record (review, interview).	FIPS 201-1, Section 2.4 - PIV Privacy Requirements
	ST-2	The information systems protect the integrity and confidentiality of transmitted information. **Assessment** *Determine that:* (i) the integrity of transmitted information is protected (interview, test, review) (ii) the confidentiality of transmitted information is protected (interview, test, review)	FIPS 201-1, Section 2.4 - PIV Privacy Requirements

		PAT = Security Management & Data Protection	
Accreditation Focus Area	Identifier	PCI Control	Source

| \multicolumn{4}{|c|}{PAT = Security Management & Data Protection} |

Accreditation Focus Area	Identifier	PCI Control	Source
Enforcement of Privacy Requirements	PR-1	Privacy act statement/notice, complaint procedures, appeals procedures for those denied identification or whose identification cards are revoked, and sanctions for employees violating privacy policies shall be developed and posted by the organization in multiple locations at the PCI facility (e.g., internet site, human resource offices, regional offices, and contractor orientation handouts). **Assessment** *Determine that:* *(i) the PCI Facility has posted privacy act statement/notice, complaint procedures, appeals procedures for those denied identification or whose identification cards are revoked, and sanctions for employees violating privacy policies (interview, review).*	OMB Memorandum 05-24
	PR-2	The organization has conducted a Privacy Impact Assessment of their PCI information system (s), compliant with Section 208 of the E-Government Act of 2002 and based on guidance found in Appendix E of OMB Memorandum 06-06. **Assessment** *Determine that:* *(i) the organization has conducted a Privacy Impact Assessment of their PCI information system (s) based on guidance found in Appendix E of OMB Memorandum 06-06 (review);* *(ii) the organization has submitted the Privacy Impact Assessment of their PCI information system (s) to OMB (interview, review).*	OMB Memorandum 05-24
	PR-3	The organization's employee and contractor identification systems of records notices (SORN's) are updated to reflect any changes in the disclosure of information to other organizations in order to be consistent with the Privacy Act of 1974 and OMB Circular A-130, Appendix 1. **Assessment** *Determine that:* *(i) the organization updates SORN's to reflect changes in the disclosure of information (review, interview).*	OMB Memorandum 05-24
	PR-4	The applicant is notified of what information in identifiable form is collected, how it will be used, what information will be disclosed and to whom, and what protections are provided to ensure the security of this information. **Assessment** *Determine that:* *(i) Before receiving the PIV Card, the PCI Facility requires the applicant to be notified of the personally identifiable information that is collected, how it will be used, what information will be disclosed and to whom, and what protections are provided to ensure the security of this information (review, observe)* *(ii) the applicant is informed of what personally identifiable information is collected, how it will be used, what information will be disclosed and to whom, and what protections are provided to ensure the security of this information (interview)*	FIPS 201-1, Section 2.4 – PIV Privacy Requirements

		PAT = Security Management & Data Protection	
Accreditation Focus Area	Identifier	PCI Control	Source
	PR-5	The PCI Facility employs technologies that allow for continuous auditing of compliance with privacy policies and practices. **Assessment** *Determine that:* *(i) the PCI Facility employs technologies that allow for the continuous auditing of compliance with privacy policies and practices. This could include the use of technology to monitor data access, data flows between information systems and the use of personally identifiable information (interview, test).*	FIPS 201-1, Section 2.4 – PIV Privacy Requirements
	PR-6	In the case of termination, any personally identifiable information that has been collected from the cardholder is disposed of in accordance with the stated privacy and data retention policies. **Assessment** *Determine that:* *(i) as a part of PIV Card termination, the organization disposes of personally identifiable information in accordance with its privacy and data retention policies (review, interview).*	FIPS 201-1, Section 5.3.2.4 – PIV Card Termination

		Infrastructure Elements	
Accreditation Focus Area	Identifier	PCI Control	Source
Deployed Products & Information Systems	DP-1	In order to be compliant with the provisions of OMB Circular A-130, App III, the PCI information system(s) are certified in accordance with NIST SP 800-37, Guide for the Security Certification and Accreditation of Federal Information Systems. **Assessment** *Determine that:* *(i) the organization has a letter showing the current accreditation decision of each information system used to support the PCI (review).*	FIPS 201-1, Appendix B.2 – Security Certification and Accreditation of IT System(s)
	DP-2	Every product utilized by a PCI facility that it falls within one of the categories listed by the GSA FIPS 201 Evaluation program, shall be listed in the GSA FIPS 201 Evaluation Program's Approved Product List (APL) **Assessment** *Determine that:* *(i) for each product that falls within one of the categories in the GSA FIPS 201 Evaluation Program, its presence (make, model, versions) is checked on the APL (review)*	OMB Memorandum 05-24
	DP-3	The organization has submitted a personalized PIV Card from their production system to GSA for testing, and it has been approved. **Assessment** *Determine that:* *(i) the organization has a letter from the GSA showing approval of the configuration of their PIV Card (review).*	OMB Memorandum 07-06

		PAT = Infrastructure Elements	
Accreditation Focus Area	Identifier	PCI Control	Source

PAT = Infrastructure Elements			
Accreditation Focus Area	Identifier	PCI Control	Source
Implementation of Credentialing Infrastructures	CI-1	For legacy Public Key Infrastructures (PKI's), the organization's CA shall be cross-certified with the Federal Bridge (FBCA) at a Medium-HW or High Assurance Level. **Assessment** *Determine that:* *the PKI is listed on the FBCA's website as being cross-certified at a Medium-HW or High Assurance Level. (review).*	FIPS 201-1, Section 5.4.4 – Migration from Legacy PKIs
	CI-2	For non-legacy PKI's, the CA that issues certificates to support PIV Card authentication participates in the hierarchical PKI for the Common Policy managed by the Federal PKI. **Assessment** *Determine that:* *(i) the PKI is listed on the Federal PKI Policy Authority's website as being a shared service provider (review).*	FIPS 201-1, Section 5.4.1 – Architecture
	CI-3	When cards are personalized, card management keys are set to be specific to each PIV Card. That is, each PIV Card shall contain a unique card management key. **Assessment** *Determine that:* *(i) the CMS vendor's documentation shows the use of unique card management keys (review);* *(ii) the OIMO indicates that card management keys are unique (interview).*	FIPS 201-1, Section 4.1.6.2 – Activation by Card Management System
	CI-4	Fingerprint images retained by organizations shall be formatted according to SP 800-76-1. **Assessment** *Determine that:* *(i) the fingerprint images are formatted according to Table 4 in SP 800-76-1 and INCITS 381 (review, test).*	SP 800-76-1, Section 3.4 – Fingerprint Template Specifications
	CI-5	Facial images collected during enrollment/identity proofing are formatted such that they conform to SP 800-76-1. **Assessment** *Determine that:* *(i) the facial images are formatted according to Table 6 in SP 800-76-1 and INCITS 385 (review, test).*	SP 800-76-1, Section 5.2 – Acquisition and Format
	CI-6	The fingerprint templates stored on the PIV Card are prepared from images of the primary and secondary fingers where the choice of fingers is based on the order of priority, as provided in FIPS 201-1, Section 4.4.1. **Assessment** *Determine that:* *(i) the procedures used to fingerprint the applicant are based on the primary and secondary finger designations as required by the standard (review, observe);* *(ii) the fingerprint templates are prepared from images of the primary and secondary fingers (test).*	SP 800-76-1, Section 3.4.1 – Source Images

PAT = Processes			
Accreditation Focus Area	Identifier	PCI Control	Source

Sponsorship Process	SP-1	A request is created in order to issue a PIV Card. **Assessment** *Determine that:* *(i) the process for making a request is documented (review);* *(ii) A PIV Request is created in order to issue a PIV Card (observe).*	FIPS 201-1, Section 2.1 – Control Objectives
	SP-2	The PCI Facility collects personal information using only forms approved by OMB under the Paperwork Reduction Act of 1995. **Assessment** *Determine that:* *(i) forms used to collect personal information have been approved by OMB (review, observe).*	OMB Memorandum 07-06

PAT = Processes			
Accreditation Focus Area	**Identifier**	**PCI Control**	**Source**
Enrollment / Identity Proofing Process	EI-1	The PCI Facility has a process in place to verify the authenticity of the source documents and match them to the identity claimed by the applicant. **Assessment** *Determine that:* *(i) the PCI Facility has a process in place to verify the authenticity of the source documents and match them to the identity claimed by the applicant (interview, observe);* *(ii) the PCI Facility has materials used to train enrollment/identity proofing officials on how to verify the authenticity of the source documents (review).*	FIPS 201-1, Section 2.1 – Control Objectives
	EI-2	The PCI Facility requires the applicant to appear in-person at least once before the issuance of a PIV Card. **Assessment** *Determine that:* *(i) the requirement that an applicant appear in-person at least once before the issuance of a PIV Card is documented (review);* *(ii) the applicant appears in-person at least once before the issuance of a PIV Card (observe).*	FIPS 201-1, Section 2.2 – PIV Identity Proofing and Registration Requirements
	EI-3	Two identity source documents are checked in accordance with the requirements of Form I-9, OMB No. 1115-0136, Employment Eligibility Verification. **Assessment** *Determine that:* *(i) the requirement to check two identity source documents in accordance with the requirements of Form I-9 is documented (review);* *(ii) two identity source documents are checked in accordance with the requirements of Form I-9 during enrollment/identity proofing (observe).*	FIPS 201-1, Section 2.2 – PIV Identity Proofing and Registration Requirements
	EI-4	One of the identity source documents used to verify the claimed identity of the applicant is a valid Federal or state government-issued photo identification. **Assessment** *Determine that:* *(i) the requirement that one of the identity source documents is a valid Federal or state government issued photo ID is documented (review);* *(ii) one of the identity source documents used to verify the claimed identity of the applicant is a valid Federal or state government-issued photo identification (observe).*	FIPS 201-1, Section 2.2 – PIV Identity Proofing and Registration Requirements

	PAT = Processes		
Accreditation Focus Area	Identifier	PCI Control	Source
	EI-5	The PCI Facility performs the entire identity proofing and enrollment/identity proofing process prior to re-issuing a PIV Card. **Assessment** *Determine that:* (i) *the requirement to perform the entire identity proofing and enrollment process prior to re-issuing a PIV Card is documented (review);* (ii) *the PCI Facility performs the entire identity proofing and enrollment process prior to re-issuing a PIV Card (observe).*	FIPS 201-1, Section 5.3.2.2 PIV Card Reissuance
	EI-6	A new facial image is collected at the time of reissuance. **Assessment** *Determine that:* (i) *the requirement to capture a new facial image is documented within the reissuance process (review);* (ii) *a new facial image is collected at the time of reissuance (observe).*	FIPS 201-1, Section 4.4 – Biometric Data Specifications
	EI-7	The biometrics (fingerprints and facial image) that are used to personalize the PIV Card must be captured during the enrollment/identity proofing process. **Assessment** *Determine that:* (i) *the requirement to capture biometrics (fingerprints and facial image) that are used to personalize the PIV Card must be captured during enrollment/identity proofing process is documented (review);* (ii) *The biometrics (fingerprints and facial image) that are used to personalize the PIV Card are captured during the enrollment/identity proofing process (observe).*	FIPS 201-1, Section 5.2 – PIV Identity Proofing and Registration Requirement
	EI-8	A cardholder waits until six weeks prior to the expiration of a valid PIV Card before applying for renewal (please note: this applies to normal renewal only and not for lost or damaged cards). **Assessment** *Determine that:* (i) *the requirement that a cardholder must wait until six weeks prior to the expiration of a valid PIV Card before applying for renewal is documented (review);* (ii) *a cardholder waits until six weeks prior to the expiration of a valid PIV Card before applying for renewal (interview).*	FIPS 201-1, Section 5.3.2.1 – PIV Card Renewal
	EI-9	The PCI Facility captures the applicant's fingerprints in accordance with any of the three imaging modes: (i) plain live scan, (ii) rolled live scan, or (iii) rolled ink card. **Assessment** (i) *the PCI Facility captures the applicant's fingerprints in accordance with any of the three imaging modes: (i) plain live scan, (ii) rolled live scan, or (iii) rolled ink card (observe).*	SP 800-76-1, Section 3.3 – Fingerprint Image Acquisition

PAT = Processes

Accreditation Focus Area	Identifier	PCI Control	Source
	EI-10	The PCI Facility has an attending official present at the time of fingerprint capture. **Assessment** *Determine that:* (i) the requirement that the PCI Facility has an attending official present at the time of fingerprint capture is documented (review); (ii) the PCI Facility has an attending official present at the time of fingerprint capture (observe).	SP 800-76-1, Section 3.3 – Fingerprint Image Acquisition
	EI-11	The PCI Facility acquires fingerprint images in accordance with Table 2 in 800-76-1. **Assessment** *Determine that:* (i) fingers are inspected for the absence of foreign materials (observe); (ii) scanner and card surfaces are clean (observe); (iii) the presentation of fingers for a plain live scan, rolled live scan, and rolled ink card are based on procedures in Table 1 (observe); (iv) multi-finger plain impression images are properly segmented into single finger images (observe).	SP 800-76-1, Section 3.3 – Fingerprint Image Acquisition
	EI-12	The PCI Facility captures the 10 fingerprints of the applicant. In the case where less than ten fingers are available, the missing fingers are labeled before transmitting to the FBI. **Assessment** *Determine that:* (i) the requirement that the PCI Facility captures the 10 fingerprints of the applicant and labels any missing fingers is documented (review); (ii) the PCI Facility captures the 10 fingerprints of the applicant and labels any missing fingers (observe).	SP 800-76-1, Section 3.3 – Fingerprint image acquisition

PAT = Processes

Accreditation Focus Area	Identifier	PCI Control	Source
Adjudication Process	AP-1	The organization conducts a National Agency Check with Written Inquiries (NACI), or other Office of Personnel Management (OPM) or National Security community investigation for each applicant for whom a successfully adjudicated NACI cannot be referenced on file. **Assessment** *Determine that:* (i) the requirement that the organization conduct a National Agency Check with Written Inquiries (NACI), or other Office of Personnel Management (OPM) or National Security community investigation for each applicant for whom a successfully adjudicated NACI cannot be referenced on file is documented (review); (ii) the organization conducts a National Agency Check with Written Inquiries (NACI), or other Office of Personnel Management (OPM) or National Security community investigation for each applicant for whom a successfully adjudicated NACI cannot be referenced on file (interview).	FIPS 201-1, Section 2.2 – PIV Identity Proofing and Registration Requirements

PAT = Processes			
Accreditation Focus Area	Identifier	PCI Control	Source
	AP-2	The organization successfully adjudicates the FBI National Criminal History Check (fingerprint check) and initiates the National Agency Check with Written Inquires (NACI) before the PIV Card is issued. **Assessment** *Determine that:* (i) *the requirement that the organization successfully adjudicates the FBI National Criminal History Check (fingerprint check) and initiates the National Agency Check with Written Inquires (NACI) before the PIV Card is issued is documented (review);* (ii) *the organization successfully adjudicates the FBI National Criminal History Check (fingerprint check) and initiates the National Agency Check with Written Inquires (NACI) before the PIV Card is issued (interview).*	FIPS 201-1, Section 2.2 – PIV Identity Proofing and Registration Requirements

PAT = Processes			
Accreditation Focus Area	Identifier	PCI Control	Source
Card Production Process	CP-1	The PIV Card implements security features that aid in reducing counterfeiting, are resistant to tampering, and provide visual evidence of tampering attempts. **Assessment** *Determine that:* (i) *the PIV Card contains at least one security feature. Examples of these security features include the following: (i) Optical varying structures, (ii) Optical varying inks, (iii) Laser etching and engraving, (iv) Holograms, (v) Holographic images, (vi) Watermarks (interview, observe).*	FIPS 201-1, Section 4.1.2 – Tamper Proofing and Resistance
	CP-2	The PIV Card is not embossed. **Assessment** *Determine that:* (i) *the PIV Card is not embossed (review, observe)*	FIPS 201-1, Section 4.1.3 – Physical Characteristics and Durability
	CP-3	Decals are not adhered to the PIV Card. **Assessment** *Determine that:* (i) *decals are not adhered to the PIV Card (review, observe).*	FIPS 201-1, Section 4.1.3 – Physical Characteristics and Durability
	CP-4	If organizations choose to punch an opening in the card body to enable the card to be worn on a lanyard, all such alterations are closely coordinated with the card vendor and/or manufacturer to ensure the card material integrity is not adversely impacted. **Assessment** *Determine that:* (i) *the integrity of a PIV Card is not affected by a punched opening (test);* (ii) *Documentation from the PIV Card vendor shows that durability and operational requirements have not been compromised (review).*	FIPS 201-1, Section 4.1.3 – Physical Characteristics and Durability

PAT = Processes

Accreditation Focus Area	Identifier	PCI Control	Source
Card Activation / Issuance Process	AI-1	The personalized PIV Card complies with all the mandatory items on the front of the PIV Card. **Assessment** *Determine that:* (i) the PIV Card meets specific requirements in FIPS 201-1 for (i)a photograph; (ii) name; (iii) employee affiliation; (iv) and expiration date (observe, test).	FIPS 201-1, Section 4.1.4.1 – Mandatory Items on the Front of the PIV Card
	AI-2	The personalized PIV Card complies with all the mandatory items on the back of the PIV Card. **Assessment** *Determine that:* (i) the PIV Card meets specific requirements in FIPS 201-1 for (i) an organization card serial number; (ii) and issuer identification (observe, test).	FIPS 201-1, Section 4.1.4.2 – Mandatory Items on the Back of the Card
	AI-3	If one or more optional items are printed on the front of the PIV Card, they comply with the requirements for the optional items on the front on the PIV Card. **Assessment** *Determine that:* (i) the PIV Card meets specific requirements in FIPS 201-1 if it includes optional items on the front of the card, such as (i) a signature; (ii) organization specific text area; (iii) rank; (iv) portable data file; (v) header; (vi) organization seal; (vii) footer; (viii) issue date; (ix) color-coding employee affiliation; (x) photo border for employee affiliation; (xi) organization-specific data (observe, test).	FIPS 201-1, Section 4.1.4.3 – Optional Items on the Front of the Card
	AI-4	If one or more optional items are printed on the back of the PIV Card, they comply with the requirements for the optional items on the back on the PIV Card. **Assessment** *Determine that:* (i) the PIV Card meets specific requirements in FIPS 201-1 if it includes optional items on the front of the card, such as (i) magnetic stripe; (ii) return to address (iii) physical characteristics of the cardholder; (iv) additional language for emergency responder officials; (v) standard Section 499, Title 18 language; (vi) linear 3 of 9 bar code; (vii) organization-specific text (zones 9 & 10) (observe, test).	FIPS 201-1, Section 4.1.4.4 – Optional Items on the Back of the Card
	AI-5	The PIV Card includes mechanisms to limit the number of PIN guesses an adversary can attempt if a card is lost or stolen. **Assessment** *Determine that:* (i) the PIV Card limits the number of incorrect PIN guesses (test, review).	FIPS 201-1, Section 4.1.6.1 – Activation by Cardholder
	AI-6	The PIV Card is valid for no more than five years. **Assessment** *Determine that:* (i) the expiration date printed on the PIV Card is no more than five years from the issuance date (observe). (ii) the expiration date is printed in the CHUID (test) (iii) the two dates (printed on the card and the expiration date in the CHUID) are the same (test)	FIPS 201-1, Section 5.3.2.1 – PIV Card Renewal

Accreditation Focus Area	Identifier	PCI Control	Source
		PAT = Processes	
	AI-7	The PCI Facility performs a 1:1 biometric match of the applicant against the biometric included in the PIV Card or in the PIV enrollment record before releasing the PIV Card to the applicant. **Assessment** *Determine that:* *(i) the requirement that the issuer performs a 1:1 biometric match of the applicant against the biometric included in the PIV Card or in the PIV enrollment record is documented (review);* *(ii) the issuer performs a 1:1 biometric match of the applicant against the biometric included in the PIV Card or in the PIV enrollment record (observe).*	FIPS 201-1, Section 5.3.1 – PIV Card Issuance
	AI-8	The PCI Facility performs a 1:1 biometric match of the PIV Card holder against the biometric included in the PIV Card prior to renewal. **Assessment** *Determine that:* *(i) the requirement that the PCI Facility performs a 1:1 biometric match of the PIV Card holder against the biometric included in the PIV Card prior to renewal is documented (review);* *(ii) the PCI Facility performs a 1:1 biometric match of the PIV Card holder against the biometric included in the PIV Card prior to renewal (observe).*	FIPS 201-1, Section 5.3.2.1 – PIV Card Renewal
	AI-9	The PCI Facility advises applicants that the PIN on the PIV Card should not be easily-guess-able or otherwise individually-identifiable in nature. **Assessment** *Determine that:* *(i) the requirement that the PCI Facility advises applicants that the PIN on the PIV Card should not be easily-guess-able or otherwise individually-identifiable in nature is documented (review);* *(ii) the PCI Facility advises applicants that the PIN on the PIV Card should not be easily-guess-able or otherwise individually-identifiable in nature (observe).*	FIPS 201-1, Section 4.1.6.1 Activation by Cardholder
	AI-10	Identity cards issued to individuals without a completed NACI or equivalent are electronically distinguishable from identity cards issued to individuals who have a completed investigation. **Assessment** *Determine that:* *(i) the PCI Facility has procedures for how to update the NACI interim indicator extension for identity cards issued to individuals without a completed NACI or equivalent (review, interview);* *(ii) for individuals without a completed NACI or equivalent, the NACI interim indicator is set to true (test);* *(iii) for individuals with a completed NACI or equivalent, the NACI interim indicator is set to false (test).*	FIPS 201-1, Section 2.2 – PIV Identity Proofing and Registration Requirements

PAT = Processes				
Accreditation Focus Area	Identifier	PCI Control	Source
	AI-11	During a PIN reset on a locked PIV Card, the PCI Facility performs a 1:1 biometric match of the PIV Card holder against the biometric included in the PIV Card prior to releasing the unlocked PIV Card back to the Card holder. **Assessment** *Determine that:* (i) the requirement that, during a PIN reset on the PIV Card, the PCI Facility performs a 1:1 biometric match of the PIV Card holder against the biometric included in the PIV Card before releasing the PIV Card is documented (review); (ii) after PIN reset on the PIV Card, the PCI Facility performs a 1:1 biometric match of the PIV Card Holder against the biometric included in the PIV before releasing the PIV Card (observe).	FIPS 201-1, Section 5.3.2.3 – PIV Card PIN Reset
	AI-12	The PCI Facility issues an electro-magnetically opaque sleeve or other protection technology to protect against any unauthorized contactless access to information stored on a PIV credential. **Assessment** *Determine that:* (i) the requirement that the PCI Facility issue an electro-magnetically opaque sleeve with every PIV Card is documented (review); (ii) the PCI Facility issues an electro-magnetically opaque sleeve with every PIV Card (interview, observe).	FIPS 201-1, Section 2.4 – Privacy Requirements
	AI-13	The organization verifies that the PIV cardholder remains in good standing, and personnel records are current before renewing/reissuing the card and associated credentials. **Assessment** *Determine that:* (i) the procedures that are followed to determine that the cardholder's records are current are documented (review); (ii) the procedures to determine the currency of the cardholder's records are followed by the PCI facility prior to renewal or reissuance of a PIV Card (observe)	FIPS 201-1, Section 5.3.2.1 – PIV Card Renewal

PAT = Processes				
Accreditation Focus Area	Identifier	PCI Control	Source
Maintenance Process	MP-1	The PIV FASC-N is not modified post-issuance. **Assessment** *Determine that:* (i) the PIV FASC-N is not modified post-issuance (review, interview).	FIPS 201-1, Section 4.2 – Cardholder Unique Identifier

\multicolumn{4}{c}{PAT = Processes}			
Accreditation Focus Area	Identifier	PCI Control	Source
	MP-2	In the case of a renewal, re-issuance and termination, the PIV Card is collected and destroyed whenever possible. **Assessment** *Determine that:* (i) *in the case of a renewal, re-issuance and termination, the requirement that the PIV Card is collected and destroyed whenever possible is documented (review);* (ii) *in the case of a renewal, re-issuance and termination, the PIV Card is collected and destroyed whenever possible (interview).*	FIPS 201-1, Section 2.3 – PIV Issuance and Maintenance Requirements
	MP-3	Normal operational procedures must be in place to ensure proper card revocation during PIV Card re-issuance and termination: (i) The PIV Card itself is revoked; (ii) Databases containing Federal Agency Smart Credential Number (FASC-N) values must be updated to reflect the change in status; (iii) The Certification Authority (CA) is informed and CRLs are updated ; and (iv) Online Certificate Status Protocol (OCSP) responders are updated so that queries with respect to certificates on the PIV Card are answered appropriately. **Assessment** *Determine that:* (i) *the PIV Card is revoked during card revocation (review, interview);* (ii) *databases containing Federal Agency Smart Credential Number (FASC-N) values must be updated to reflect the change in status (interview);* (iii) *the CA is informed and the revoked certificates on the PIV Card are placed on the CRL (test, review);* (iv) *online Certificate Status Protocol (OCSP) responders are updated (test, review).*	FIPS 201-1 Section 5.3.2.4 PIV Card Termination
	MP-4	If the PIV Card cannot be collected and destroyed, normal operating procedures are completed within 18 hours of notification. **Assessment** *Determine that:* (i) *documentation includes the requirement that if PIV Card cannot be collected and destroyed, normal operating procedures are completed within 18 hours of notification (review);* (ii) *if the PIV Card cannot be collected and destroyed, normal operating procedures are completed within 18 hours of notification (observe).*	FIPS 201-1, Section 5.3.2.2 – PIV Card Reissuance
	MP-5	Upon PIV Card termination, the organization enforces a standard methodology of updating systems of records to indicate employee termination, and this status is distributed effectively throughout systems used for physical and logical access to organization facilities and resources. **Assessment** *Determine that:* (i) *the PCI Facility has documented its procedures for updating information systems to indicate employee termination (review);* (ii) *the PCI Facility updates information systems to indicate employee termination (interview, observe).*	FIPS 201-1, Section 5.3.2 - PIV Card Maintenance
	MP-6	The organization posts a quarterly report, to the organization's website, stating the number of PIV Cards issued to date, and the link is emailed to OMB.	OMB Memorandum 07-06

		PAT = Processes	
Accreditation Focus Area	Identifier	PCI Control	Source
		Assessment *Determine that:* (i) *the organization develops and posts a quarterly report to the organization's website according to the requirements of the attachment to OMB memorandum 07-06 (review);* (ii) *the organization sends the link to the report to OMB on a quarterly basis (review, interview).*	
	MP-7	The organization has completed a lifecycle walkthrough at one year intervals since the last accreditation date, and the results are documented in a report to the DAA. **Assessment** *Determine that:* (i) *the organization has completed a lifecycle walkthrough to cover sponsorship, enrollment/identity proofing, card production, card activation/issuance and maintenance processes (interview);* (ii) *a lifecycle walkthrough has been completed at one year intervals since the last accreditation date (interview);* (iii) *the results of the PCI lifecycle walkthrough have been documented and reviewed by the DAA (review, interview).*	SP 800-79-1, Section 5.4 - Monitoring Phase

APPENDIX H: ASSESSMENT AND ACCREDITATION TASKS FOR PIV CARD ISSUERS (PCIs)

Phases, Tasks, and Sub-tasks	Person(s) Responsible
Initiation Phase	
Task 1: Preparation	
Subtask 1.1: Confirm that the PCI and its operations have been fully described and documented in the PCI's operations plan.	OIMO
Subtask 1.2: Confirm that processes conducted by the PCI Facility are in accordance with the policies and procedures specified in the PCI operations plan and are documented in Standard Operating Procedures.	OIMO, PCIF Manager
Task 2: Resource Identification	
Subtask 2.1: Identify the Senior Authorizing Official (SAO), Designated Accreditation Authority (DAA), Privacy Official (PO), PCIF Managers, Assessor, and other key personnel at the facility level, who are performing functions such as enrollment/identity proofing, card production, and card activation/issuance.	OIMO
Subtask 2.2: Determine the accreditation boundary for the PCI.	OIMO, DAA
Subtask 2.3: Determine the resources and the time needed for the accreditation of the PCI, and prepare for execution of the assessment.	OIMO, DAA
Task 3: Operations Plan Analysis and Acceptance	
Subtask 3.1: Review the list of required PCI controls documented in the organization's PCI operation plan to confirm that they have been implemented properly.	DAA, OIMO
Subtask 3.2: Analyze the PCI operations plan to determine if there are deficiencies in satisfying all the policies, procedures, and other requirements in FIPS 201-1 that could result in a DATO being issued.	DAA, OIMO
Subtask 3.3: Verify that the PCI operations plan is acceptable.	DAA
Assessment Phase	

Phases, Tasks, and Sub-tasks	Person(s) Responsible
Task 4: PCI Control Assessment	
Subtask 4.1: Review the suggested and selected assessment methods for each PCI control in preparation for the assessment.	Assessor
Subtask 4.2: Assemble all documentation and supporting materials necessary for the assessment of the PCI; if these documents include previous assessments, review the findings and determine if they are applicable to the current assessment.	OIMO, Assessor
Subtask 4.3: Assess the required PCI controls using the prescribed assessment procedures found in Appendix G.	Assessor
Subtask 4.4: Prepare the assessment report.	Assessor
Task 5: Assessment Documentation	
Subtask 5.1: Provide the OIMO with the assessment report.	Assessor
Subtask 5.2: Revise the PCI operations plan (if necessary) and implement its new provisions.	OIMO
Subtask 5.3: Prepare the corrective actions plan (CAP).	OIMO
Subtask 5.4: Assemble the accreditation submission package and submit to the DAA.	OIMO
Accreditation Phase	
Task 6: Accreditation Decision	
Subtask 6.1: Review the assessment decision package to see if it is complete and that all applicable PCI controls have been fully assessed using the designated assessment procedures.	DAA
Subtask 6.2: Determine that the risk to the organization's operations, assets, or potentially affected individuals is acceptable, that the PCI controls have been adequately assessed and prepare the final accreditation decision letter	DAA
Task 7: Accreditation Documentation	
Subtask 7.1: Provide copies of the final accreditation package, in either paper or electronic form, to the OIMO and any other organization officials having interests, roles, or responsibilities in the PCI	DAA

Phases, Tasks, and Sub-tasks	Person(s) Responsible
Subtask 7.2: Update the PCI's operations plan.	OIMO

Monitoring Phase

Task 8: Operations Plan Update	
Subtask 8.1: Document all relevant changes in the PCI within the operations plan	OIMO
Subtask 8.2: Analyze the proposed or actual changes to the PCI, and determine the impact of such changes.	OIMO
Task 9: Annual Lifecycle Walkthrough	
Subtask 9.1: Observe all the processes involved in getting a PIV Card, including those from sponsorship to maintenance. Observe each process, and compare its controls against the applicable list of required PCI controls. If a PCI has several facilities, this process should be repeated using randomly selected PCIFs.	OIMO (or designated appointee)
Subtask 9.2: The results of the lifecycle walkthrough are summarized in a report to the DAA. Deficiencies must be highlighted along with corrective actions that must be implemented to correct any deficiencies.	OIMO, DAA

www.ingramcontent.com/pod-product-compliance
Lightning Source LLC
Chambersburg PA
CBHW081839170526
45167CB00007B/2839